PALMA DE MALLORCA

TRAVEL GUIDE 2025-2026

Discover Historic Architecture, Sun-Soaked Beaches, Culture, Local Markets, Luxury Hotels, Hidden Gems, Local Culinary Favorites, and Everything You Need for an Unforgettable Getaway.

ALL RIGHTS RESERVED

DISCLAIMER

This book, *Palma de Mallorca Travel Guide 2025–2026*, is intended for informational and educational purposes only. While every effort has been made to ensure the accuracy and timeliness of the content at the time of publication, the author and publisher make no representations or warranties regarding the completeness, currentness, suitability, or validity of any information presented. Changes in business operations, local laws, travel advisories, prices, schedules, and contact details may occur without notice.

The inclusion of specific businesses, accommodations, restaurants, or attractions is for informational purposes only and does not constitute an endorsement or guarantee of quality or availability. Readers are encouraged to verify details independently before making travel arrangements.

The author and publisher are not liable for any loss, injury, inconvenience, or damage resulting from the use of this guide or reliance upon the information contained herein. Travel involves inherent risks, and all readers are advised to make responsible decisions and consult official sources where appropriate.

All trademarks, product names, and logos mentioned in this book are the property of their respective owners. Their use does not imply affiliation with or endorsement by the author or publisher.

This guide is an original work and may not be reproduced, distributed, or transmitted in any form without prior written permission from the publisher, except in the case of brief quotations used in reviews or academic citations.

TABLE OF CONTENT

Chapter 1. Introduction to Palma de Mallorca   **5**

    1.1 Overview of the City   5

    1.2 Brief History and Culture   8

    1.3 Why Visit Palma in 2025–2026   11

    1.4 Travel Seasons and Best Times to Go   14

Chapter 2. Planning Your Trip   **18**

    2.1 Entry Requirements and Travel Documents   18

    2.2 Getting to Palma de Mallorca   22

    2.3 Transportation Within the City   25

    2.4 Travel Tips and Local Etiquette   29

Chapter 3. Top Attractions in Palma   **34**

    3.1 Bellver Castle (Castell de Bellver)   34

    3.2 Royal Palace of La Almudaina (Palacio Real de La Almudaina)   37

    3.3 Palma Old Town (Casco Antiguo)   40

    3.4 Es Baluard Museum of Modern & Contemporary Art   44

    3.5 Playa de Palma & the City Beaches   47

    3.6 Arab Baths (Banys Àrabs)   51

Chapter 4. Neighborhoods and Districts   **54**

    4.1 Old Town (Casco Antiguo)   54

    4.2 Santa Catalina   57

    4.3 El Molinar and Portixol   61

    4.4 La Lonja and Paseo Marítimo   64

Chapter 5. Where to Stay   **68**

    5.1 Luxury Hotels and Boutique Stays   68

    5.2 Mid-Range and Family-Friendly Options   70

    5.3 Budget-Friendly Hotels and Hostels   74

    5.4 Best Areas to Stay for Different Travelers   78

Chapter 6. Food and Drink Scene   **82**

    6.1 Traditional Mallorcan Dishes   82

    6.2 Best Restaurants and Tapas Bars   85

    6.3 Local Markets and Street Food   89

    6.4 Wine, Cocktails, and Café Culture   92

Chapter 7. Outdoor Activities and Beaches   **1**

    7.1 Top Beaches Around Palma   1

    7.2 Cycling and Walking Routes   1

    7.3 Boat Tours and Water Sports   1

    7.4 Parks and Green Spaces   1

Chapter 8: Day Trips and Excursions   **1**

    8.1 Valldemossa   1

8.2 Sóller and Port de Sóller 1

8.3 Serra de Tramuntana 1

Chapter 9. Shopping and Local Products **1**

9.1 Markets and Artisan Goods 1

9.2 Best Streets for Boutique Shopping 1

9.3 Local Souvenirs and What to Buy 1

9.4 Mallorcan Fashion and Craft 1

Chapter 10. Practical Information & Appendix **1**

10.1 Currency, Costs, and Budgeting 1

10.2 Language, Safety, and Emergency Info 1

10.3 Accessibility and Family Travel 1

10.4 Useful Contacts and Resources 1

Chapter 1. Introduction to Palma de Mallorca

1.1 Overview of the City

Palma de Mallorca, the vibrant capital of Spain's Balearic Islands, is a city that manages to strike an effortless balance between centuries-old charm and a distinctly modern Mediterranean spirit. Sitting right on the bay of Palma and backed by the dramatic Serra de Tramuntana mountain range, the city has evolved from its ancient roots into a destination that offers both rich cultural depth and easygoing coastal living.

This isn't just a beach town with pretty architecture—it's a layered place, full of stories. Palma has been shaped by Romans, Moors, and Christian monarchs, and that layered past is still very much alive in its streets. Gothic spires loom above palm-fringed promenades, Arab baths hide in quiet courtyards, and modern art museums sit inside old military fortresses. Walk just a few blocks and you'll pass sandstone mansions, open-air cafés, working harbors, and family-run bakeries filled with ensaïmadas (a local pastry you'll see everywhere).

With a population of around 400,000, Palma isn't overwhelmingly large, but it's big enough to feel like a real city—one that locals live in year-round, not just a resort town catering to tourists.

That means it has a pulse. There's a strong culinary scene that goes well beyond paella and tapas, a healthy mix of high-end shopping and quirky markets, and neighborhoods with distinct personalities, each offering something a little different.

A City with Many Faces

One of the most intriguing things about Palma is how its personality changes depending on where you are and what time of day you're exploring. Early mornings in the Old Town feel almost cinematic—quiet alleys, dappled sunlight, and the occasional clatter of delivery carts echoing off the stone. Come midday, the squares fill with chatter and clinking glasses as locals and visitors crowd into shaded terraces for long lunches.

Head down to the waterfront and you'll see an entirely different scene: sleek yachts bobbing in the marina, joggers along the promenade, and a mix of families, cyclists, and retirees strolling past. A bit farther east, you'll hit the city beaches—clean, well-maintained, and filled with a casual crowd of swimmers and sunbathers.

In the evening, the energy shifts again. Restaurants light up, bars come alive, and the backstreets of neighborhoods like Santa Catalina buzz with conversation and music. Despite the movement, there's a calmness to the rhythm of daily life here. It's lively, but never frantic.

Cultural and Architectural Tapestry

Palma's architectural mix is part of what makes it so fascinating to explore. The city's centerpiece is **La Seu**, the massive Gothic cathedral that dominates the waterfront skyline. Built on the site of a former mosque, it's a powerful symbol of the island's past—and Gaudí even had a hand in its redesign during the early 20th century. From there, history fans can walk just a few steps to **Palau de l'Almudaina**, a royal palace with roots in Islamic rule.

As you go deeper into the city, you'll find well-preserved medieval streets, beautiful courtyards hidden behind wrought-iron gates, and Art Nouveau facades that feel straight out of Barcelona. Even the newer parts of the city show a strong design sense—Palma doesn't do "ugly urban sprawl." Instead, it manages to feel cohesive, elegant, and undeniably Mediterranean.

But it's not just about what's old. Modern Palma embraces the arts, design, and creativity. Contemporary galleries like **Es Baluard** bring a fresh voice to the historic heart of the city, and cultural festivals—ranging from classical music to street theater—dot the calendar all year long.

A Place to Live, Not Just Visit

Perhaps what makes Palma stand out most is that it's not just built for visitors. Sure, tourism is a major part of the economy, but the city is also home to a diverse population—artists, entrepreneurs, students, retirees from all over Europe, and lifelong locals who've seen the city grow and evolve. The infrastructure reflects that: great schools, efficient public transport, bike lanes, community markets, and healthcare centers. You'll find real neighborhoods with grocery stores, tailors, pharmacies, and little cafés where baristas know their regulars by name.

This balance between tourism and local life gives Palma an authenticity that many coastal cities have lost. It's a place you can settle into. Spend a week here, and you'll start recognizing faces. Spend a month, and you'll know your favorite café, your go-to bakery, and the best place to watch the sunset.

Gateway to the Rest of Mallorca

While Palma itself is packed with things to see and do, it also serves as a gateway to the rest of the island. Major roads, trains, and bus routes all radiate out from the city, making it easy to explore the scenic countryside, coastal villages, vineyards, and mountain towns that give Mallorca its full character. That convenience makes Palma a perfect base—whether you're here for a few days or several weeks.

And because the island is relatively compact, you can have breakfast at a seaside café in Palma, hike a cliffside trail near Deià by midday, and be back in town in time for dinner with your feet in the sand.

Palma in 2025–2026

Looking ahead, Palma continues to evolve in thoughtful ways. Sustainability is becoming a real focus, with efforts to reduce over-tourism, promote green travel, and preserve the city's historic core. More pedestrian zones are being created, bike-share programs expanded, and support for local businesses continues to grow.

New boutique hotels and cultural spaces are opening, but in ways that blend into the city's identity rather than changing it. The emphasis isn't on building bigger or flashier—it's on enhancing the quality of what's already here. That approach makes the city feel both fresh and grounded, ideal for travelers who want something a little deeper than the typical tourist circuit.

In short: Palma de Mallorca isn't just a pretty postcard of a place. It's layered, lively, deeply historic, and yet still full of life. Whether you're here for the sun and sand or the food and history—or all of it—it's a city that feels both welcoming and worth knowing better.

1.2 Brief History and Culture

Palma's history isn't just tucked away in museums or plaques on old buildings—it's part of everyday life. You see it in the design of the streets, in the names of neighborhoods, in the customs that locals still observe, and in the stone walls that have watched over the city for centuries. To understand Palma today, it helps to take a step back and see how this city on the coast of Mallorca has been shaped by waves of civilization, conquest, trade, and reinvention.

From Prehistoric Settlements to Roman Foundation

Long before Palma had cathedrals or cobbled streets, the area was home to the Talaiotic people—prehistoric settlers whose stone-built structures can still be seen across the island. They left behind burial sites, watchtowers, and remnants of early communities that give us clues about life on Mallorca before the classical era.

The Romans arrived around 123 BCE under the command of Quintus Caecilius Metellus, who conquered the island and founded the city they called **Palmaria**. As with most Roman towns, it was laid out in a grid, with public baths, temples, and an organized center. Though the ancient Roman Palma wasn't especially large, it served as a strategic outpost and trading hub in the Mediterranean. Remnants of Roman life—fragments of mosaics, pottery, and walls—have been uncovered in the city center, quietly reminding us of this early chapter.

Moorish Influence: A City Transformed

In 902 CE, the Moors took control of the island, marking the start of a significant cultural shift. They called the city **Medina Mayurqa**, and it flourished as a bustling Islamic city for nearly 300 years. This era brought sophisticated irrigation systems, agriculture, science, and art. Palma became known for its trade routes, vibrant markets, and cosmopolitan population.

It's during this period that many of Palma's lasting features took shape—especially its layout. The tangle of narrow, winding alleys in the Old Town reflects the classic design of Islamic cities, built to offer shade and privacy. Several structures from this era still stand, the most famous being the **Banys Àrabs** (Arab Baths), one of the oldest and best-preserved buildings in Palma. Simple and elegant, they're a rare and precious window into that time.

The Christian Reconquest and the Gothic Era

In 1229, King James I of Aragon conquered Mallorca during the Christian reconquest of the Iberian Peninsula. Medina Mayurqa was renamed Palma once again, and the city underwent major changes. Churches and palaces rose where mosques had once stood. New institutions were established, and the city's skyline began to shift.

The most dramatic of those additions was **La Seu**, Palma's massive Gothic cathedral, which took more than 300 years to complete. Built directly on the site of the city's main mosque, the cathedral became both a symbol of Christian rule and a masterpiece of Mediterranean Gothic architecture. Nearby, **Palau de l'Almudaina**—a former Islamic fortress—was reimagined as a royal residence.

This period saw the rise of Palma as a major port city in the Crown of Aragon. The combination of military power, religious devotion, and flourishing trade gave the city a mix of strength and sophistication that would define it for centuries.

Turmoil, Piracy, and Recovery

From the late 14th through the 17th centuries, Palma experienced its fair share of troubles. Pirate raids were a constant threat, and political instability on the mainland often spilled over onto the island. The city built defensive walls and towers, many of which still stand today. Despite the tension, commerce continued, and Palma remained an important link in the chain of Mediterranean trade.

During the Spanish Habsburg period, the city saw waves of wealth and hardship. Epidemics, famines, and economic slumps hit hard, but so did periods of rebuilding and cultural investment. Baroque churches, new convents, and grand merchant houses sprang up. The city grew slowly but steadily, adapting to the times.

Modernization and the 20th Century

Like much of Spain, Palma entered the modern age gradually. The 19th century brought political change, industrial development, and a growing awareness of Mallorca's potential as a cultural destination. Train lines were built, urban plans were drawn, and public squares opened up. The old city began to stretch and modernize, but without losing its historic soul.

In the 20th century, especially after the Spanish Civil War, Palma began to transform more dramatically. Tourism took off in the 1950s and '60s, with travelers drawn to the island's beaches, warm weather, and charm. Mass tourism brought both prosperity and challenges. Historic sites were preserved, but some development went unchecked. Still, Palma managed to avoid many of the pitfalls that overran other tourist cities.

By the 1990s and early 2000s, Palma was actively reinventing itself—not just as a sun-and-sea destination, but as a cultural capital. Restoration projects, public art installations, and cultural festivals breathed new life into old spaces.

Cultural Identity: More than One Story

Today, Palma is a cultural crossroads. It's distinctly Mallorcan but also very much international. Walk through the city and you'll hear Catalan (specifically Mallorquín), Castilian Spanish, German, English, and a dozen other languages in the span of a few blocks. This blend of identities is part of what makes Palma so dynamic.

Local culture is still deeply rooted in tradition. Seasonal festivals like **Sant Sebastià** and **Semana Santa** bring locals together in celebration, with fireworks, parades, and rituals that have been carried out for generations. Markets like **Mercat de l'Olivar** and

Santa Catalina don't just sell food—they reflect a way of life. Crafts like ceramics, leatherwork, and embroidery are still practiced, and family-run businesses are the backbone of daily commerce.

At the same time, Palma has a creative, forward-looking spirit. There's a thriving art scene, a passion for design and architecture, and a growing interest in sustainability and slow living. Young chefs are reimagining traditional recipes. Musicians and designers are putting down roots. And people from all over the world are choosing to call the city home—not just for its beauty, but for its quality of life.

In essence, Palma's history isn't something you read about in books—it's something you walk through. It's there in the shadows of cathedral arches, the spice-scented breeze from a bakery, the festivals that fill the squares, and the stories locals still pass down. The past is never far away, but it never weighs the city down. Palma moves forward while keeping its roots deep.

1.3 Why Visit Palma in 2025–2026

Let's get right to it—Palma is one of those rare places that manages to hit the sweet spot between laid-back island living and cosmopolitan buzz. It's coastal, historic, stylish, and surprisingly soulful. And if you've been thinking about making the trip in 2025 or 2026, you're choosing the perfect window. The city is hitting its stride in ways that feel both exciting and intentional—there's more art, better food, cleaner infrastructure, and a deeper awareness of what makes the island special in the first place.

Whether you're chasing sun, food, culture, or just a slower rhythm of life, Palma isn't going to disappoint.

The Weather Plays Along

Let's start with the obvious: the climate. Palma has the kind of weather people move for. Long, bright summers stretch from late May into early October, and even the winters are gentle. Sure, you might need a jacket in January, but snow? Not here. Sunshine dominates the forecast year-round, and the Mediterranean breeze keeps it from ever feeling too oppressive. The shoulder seasons—spring and early fall—are absolute magic. Fewer tourists, golden light, and enough warmth to swim in the sea. If you're looking for that just-right time to go, late April to early June and September into mid-October are golden.

A City That Feels Like a Resort (But Isn't)

Palma isn't a resort town—but it does have that easy, vacation-friendly vibe. The palm-lined promenade, the yacht-filled harbor, the beaches just minutes from the old city—everything's set up to help you unwind. Yet you're never far from a boutique, a gallery, a wine bar, or a centuries-old landmark.

This is part of Palma's charm. It's not pretending to be anything—it simply is. A working city with a rich cultural fabric and a lifestyle that blends siestas, market runs, and espresso breaks with sunsets by the water. You'll find luxury here if that's what you're after, but you'll also find authenticity: family-owned cafés, old fishermen unloading their catch, and musicians playing in the alleyways after dark.

A Cultural Scene That's Not Just for Show

There's real substance beneath the surface in Palma. The city has been doubling down on its cultural identity over the past few years, and it shows. The **Es Baluard Museum of Contemporary Art** is no longer just a local secret—it's become a centerpiece, drawing in artists and curators from across Europe. Smaller galleries and studios are cropping up in every corner of the Old Town.

Live music, pop-up art events, independent film screenings—there's something happening almost every night if you know where to look. And the best part? You don't need to be a highbrow culture snob to enjoy it. This is accessible, alive, and very human. The city's cultural pulse is more about passion than polish.

Food That's Getting Better by the Bite

Mallorca has always had good food, but Palma is taking it to another level. Traditional Mallorcan dishes like , *sobrasada*, and *ensaimada* still hold their ground—and rightly so—but now you'll find chefs putting modern spins on local ingredients in ways that are genuinely exciting.

The city's markets are at the center of this food revival. Walk through **Mercat de Santa Catalina** or **Mercat de l'Olivar**, and you'll see what we mean. Fresh seafood, local cheeses, hand-pressed olive oil, seasonal produce—it's a daily reminder that Mallorca's land and sea are still deeply generous.

What's changed in recent years is the rise of a younger, more experimental food scene. Think wine bars with natural vintages from local growers. Farm-to-table spots tucked into 14th-century courtyards. Tasting menus that manage to be both creative and deeply rooted in place. Whether you're grabbing tapas with your toes still sandy or booking a table for something more refined, Palma delivers.

Beaches, Yes. But So Much More

Sure, Palma has beaches—you don't have to leave the city limits to sink your toes in the sand. But what makes it stand out is that the beach is just *one* part of the story. You could start your day with a swim, wander through an art exhibit mid-morning, have lunch at a terrace with cathedral views, spend the afternoon hiking just outside town, and still catch sunset cocktails by the marina.

There's also easy access to the rest of the island. Rent a bike or a car, and within an hour, you're deep in the mountains, exploring hidden coves, or discovering sleepy inland villages where time seems to have hit pause.

2025–2026: The Right Time to Go

These next couple of years are ideal for visiting. Why? Well, Palma is evolving—but carefully. City leaders are working on sustainability measures to manage tourism, protect the coastline, and preserve the local lifestyle. There's an increased focus on responsible travel—more walking routes, better public transport, and support for local artisans and food producers.

Infrastructure has improved too. Wi-Fi is fast, roads are in great shape, and English is widely spoken—though if you try a little Spanish or Mallorquín, you'll earn instant respect. Flights from across Europe are frequent and affordable. And with the global travel world still recalibrating post-pandemic, there's a renewed appreciation for places that offer both cultural richness and room to breathe.

Palma is that place. Not overwhelmed, not artificial, not on auto-pilot.

Who Is Palma For?

Honestly? Just about everyone. It's a solo traveler's dream—safe, walkable, and full of places to meet people without trying too hard. Couples love it for the romance, the views, the slow dinners under string lights. Families find it surprisingly kid-friendly, with beaches, parks, and short distances between attractions. And digital nomads? They're setting up base here in growing numbers, drawn by the mix of work-life balance and lifestyle perks.

Palma has this rare flexibility. You can build the trip you want—lazy, lively, culture-packed, or totally unplugged.

So why visit Palma in 2025–2026?

Because it's that rare kind of city where you can wake up to church bells, have lunch by the sea, explore centuries of history, and still be barefoot by sunset. It's small enough to feel personal, yet big enough to keep surprising you. And most of all, it's a place that's proud of what it is—quietly confident, impossibly charming, and absolutely worth the journey.

1.4 Travel Seasons and Best Times to Go

Timing your trip to Palma de Mallorca can make all the difference. This isn't a one-season destination—it's more like a rotating carousel of moods, each with its own perks, quirks, and vibe. Whether you're after beach weather, crowd-free streets, or cultural events, there's a sweet spot that matches your travel style. The key is knowing what each season brings and what trade-offs to expect.

Let's break it down.

Spring (March to May)

The season of soft light, blooming orange trees, and sweet temperatures.

If there's a season Palma wears best, it might be spring. The city shakes off winter's sleepiness and returns to life—but without the summer frenzy. The beaches start to fill (especially by late April), cafés spill onto sidewalks again, and the sun hangs around just long enough to let you linger.

Weather: Temperatures range from the upper 50s °F (around 15°C) in March to mid-70s °F (about 24°C) by May. Rain is possible, but it's usually brief.

What's great:

- Flowers everywhere, especially almond blossoms inland
- Lower hotel prices and fewer crowds
- Outdoor dining becomes a thing again
- Perfect time for cycling, hiking, or day trips

What to watch for: The sea's still a little brisk in March and early April—not exactly beach-swimming territory unless you're brave.

Summer (June to August)

This is when Palma hits its high note—and the thermostat.

Summer in Palma is bold, bright, and very much alive. The city fills with travelers from across Europe, and the beaches feel like they've been scooped straight out of a postcard. It's peak season in every way—sunshine, festivals, nightlife, and yes, tourists.

Weather: Think long, hot days averaging 85°F (29°C), with plenty of sun and very little rain. The sea is warm and dreamy by mid-June onward.

What's great:

- Beach weather, hands down
- Festivals like **Nit de Sant Joan** (June 23)—bonfires on the beach, fireworks, dancing until sunrise
- Vibrant nightlife, rooftop bars, and summer markets
- Easy ferry hops to neighboring islands like Menorca or Ibiza

What to watch for:

- Crowds—especially in July and August
- Higher hotel prices
- Some locals take their holidays in August, and a few smaller shops or eateries may close

If you're a social traveler who loves warm nights, open-air dining, and that buzz in the air, summer's your time.

Autumn (September to November)

The locals call this their favorite season—and for good reason.

Fall in Palma feels like an encore to summer, but without the noise. September still brings warm days and swimmable seas, while October slips gently into cooler breezes and a more relaxed rhythm. By November, it's quieter—but not dull. This is when Palma shows off its everyday beauty without the spotlight.

Weather: September's still toasty (high 70s to low 80s °F / 25–27°C), but by November, you're looking at cooler mid-60s °F (17–19°C). Expect the occasional rain shower in October and November.

What's great:

- Smaller crowds but summer-style weather through September
- Harvest season—local wine and olive oil festivals start up
- Perfect for cultural travelers, food lovers, or those craving peace
- Hotel rates drop after September

What to watch for:

- Shorter days by late October
- Swimming still possible early in the season, but by November, it's mostly for the brave

Winter (December to February)

Quiet, calm, and surprisingly lovely—if you know what you're getting.

Winter in Palma doesn't scream "vacation" the way summer does, but that's exactly the point. It's when the city feels most authentic. You won't be sunbathing, but you can stroll through near-empty streets, visit galleries with breathing room, and catch a very different side of island life.

Weather: Mild and manageable—highs in the low 60s °F (16–18°C), with chilly mornings and the occasional rainy day. Snow is almost unheard of in Palma itself.

What's great:

- Peaceful streets, fewer tourists
- Lower prices across the board
- Local festivals like **Sant Sebastià** in January—fire runs, concerts, and city-wide parties
- Cozy cafés and holiday decorations in the Old Town

What to watch for:

- Some resorts and beach clubs shut down until spring
- Shorter daylight hours

- Not beach weather, obviously—but still good for walking and sightseeing

When's the Best Time to Go, Really?

Here's the short answer: **late April to early June** or **mid-September through October**.

You get sunshine, fewer crowds, better prices, and all the charm of Palma without the heatwave or high-season energy drain. It's ideal for walking the city, biking along the coast, hitting museums, and still fitting in a beach day or two.

But if you're after nonstop sunshine, music-filled nights, and lively energy? July and August will deliver that in full. Just be ready to share the magic with plenty of others.

And if your style is more peaceful mornings, local markets, and crisp walks through ancient alleyways, the off-season might surprise you in the best way.

One Last Thing...

No matter when you go, Palma gives you something worth remembering. Some cities depend on a season to shine. Palma? It simply shifts gears. Whether you're sipping wine in a warm courtyard in May or wandering the cathedral steps on a bright December afternoon, there's always something quietly beautiful waiting to be noticed.

Chapter 2. Planning Your Trip

2.1 Entry Requirements and Travel Documents

Before you start daydreaming about tapas, turquoise coves, and golden sunsets over the harbor, there's one crucial thing to handle first—getting into Spain. While Palma de Mallorca is part of the Balearic Islands, it follows the same entry regulations as mainland Spain. So whether you're flying in from New York, Berlin, or Buenos Aires, your passport and paperwork need to be sorted before that boarding pass gets scanned.

Let's break down everything you need to know about visas, passports, and border control—without making it feel like a bureaucratic jungle.

Passport Requirements

For all travelers:
You'll need a valid passport to enter Palma de Mallorca. This is non-negotiable, even for short stays. The Spanish authorities require that your passport:

- Be **valid for at least three months** beyond your planned date of departure from the Schengen Area
- Be issued **within the last 10 years**

Tip: Some travelers don't realize that the "10 years" rule is separate from the expiration date. Even if your passport hasn't expired yet, it must not be older than 10 years from the date it was issued.

Who Needs a Visa?

Spain is part of the **Schengen Area**, a zone of 27 European countries with shared border and visa rules. Whether or not you need a visa depends on your nationality and the length of your stay.

Visa-Free Entry (Tourist Stays Up to 90 Days)

Citizens of over 60 countries can enter Spain (and thus Palma) without a visa for short visits. This includes travelers from:

- **United States**
- **Canada**
- **United Kingdom**
- **Australia**
- **New Zealand**
- **Most Latin American countries**
- **Japan and South Korea**

You can stay for **up to 90 days in any 180-day period** for tourism, business, or family visits. Just make sure you haven't overstayed in any other Schengen country recently—your 90 days are counted cumulatively across the entire zone.

Who *Does* Need a Visa?

If you're from a country that's not on the visa-exempt list (such as India, China, South Africa, or most African and some Southeast Asian nations), you'll need to apply for a **Schengen short-stay visa (Type C)** before arriving.

Apply through your nearest Spanish consulate or embassy. Processing can take anywhere from two weeks to over a month, so plan ahead.

Coming Soon: ETIAS (for Visa-Exempt Travelers)

Starting in **mid-2025**, travelers from visa-exempt countries (like the U.S., U.K., and Canada) will need to apply for **ETIAS**—a new **pre-travel electronic authorization system**, similar to the U.S. ESTA.

It's not a visa, but you'll need it to enter any Schengen country. Here's what we know:

- Cost: €7 (free for travelers under 18 and over 70)
- Valid for three years or until your passport expires
- Expected to be fast and done entirely online

Bottom line: If you're traveling to Palma in late 2025 or 2026, double-check the ETIAS rollout status and make sure to apply at least a few days before your trip.

Other Important Entry Documents

Regardless of whether you need a visa or not, Spanish border agents may ask for:

- **Proof of onward travel** (such as a return ticket)
- **Proof of accommodation** (hotel reservation or address where you're staying)
- **Proof of sufficient funds** (€100 per day is the general benchmark)
- **Travel insurance** (not always checked, but highly recommended)

They don't ask every traveler for these—but they *can*. Better to be ready than risk being delayed or, worse, denied entry.

Special Rules for EU/EEA/Swiss Citizens

If you're a citizen of an EU country, Iceland, Norway, Liechtenstein, or Switzerland, you're in the easiest category. You don't need a visa, and you can enter Palma with a valid national ID card—no passport required. You also won't be subject to any ETIAS requirements.

Arriving via Other Schengen Countries

Palma has a well-connected international airport (PMI), but many travelers arrive after flying into larger hubs like Barcelona, Madrid, or even Paris, then connecting to Mallorca via a domestic flight.

If that's your route, **your passport will be checked at your first point of entry into the Schengen Area**—not necessarily in Palma. So don't be surprised if you land in Mallorca and walk right into baggage claim without any passport stamping.

Traveling with Children

If you're traveling with minors, Spain takes child travel documentation seriously. Make sure:

- Kids have their **own passports**
- If a child is traveling with only one parent or a guardian, **bring a notarized letter of consent** from the non-traveling parent
- Adopted children or children with a different last name than their guardian may be asked to provide proof of relationship

Overstaying Your Visa or 90-Day Limit

This is where travelers sometimes get into trouble. Even one day over the 90-day limit can lead to:

- Fines
- Entry bans
- Issues with future travel in Europe

Keep track of your days. If you're traveling around Europe, remember that days spent in France, Germany, or Italy *also count* toward your Schengen total.

If you're planning a longer stay in Palma for study, work, retirement, or anything beyond tourism, you'll need to apply for the proper **long-stay visa (Type D)** through a Spanish consulate before you arrive.

A Word on Brexit (for UK Travelers)

Since the U.K. is no longer part of the EU, British citizens can no longer stay indefinitely in Spain. As of now:

- You get up to **90 days in any 180-day period**
- Your passport must meet the **3-month validity** and **less-than-10-years-old** rules
- ETIAS will apply from 2025

Local Entry Tips and Airport Customs

At Palma's **Son Sant Joan Airport (PMI)**, immigration usually runs smoothly, but lines can get long during peak hours. Have your documents ready and filled out. Customs agents aren't usually heavy-handed, but they may screen for:

- Large cash amounts (over €10,000 must be declared)
- Restricted food items, especially meats and dairy from outside the EU
- Drones, professional camera gear, or anything that looks like it might require a permit

Final Checklist Before You Fly

- Passport valid for 3+ months past your trip
- Know if you need a visa or ETIAS
- Return or onward flight booked
- Accommodation address saved
- Travel insurance in place
- Supporting documents (just in case)

That's it for the red tape. Once you're past that border control desk, the only thing you need to worry about is which tapas bar to hit first.

2.2 Getting to Palma de Mallorca

Reaching Palma de Mallorca is easier than many travelers expect. Thanks to its popularity as a Mediterranean holiday destination, the island is well connected by air and sea, with seasonal boosts that ramp up access during the warmer months. Whether you're flying in from another European capital, taking a ferry from mainland Spain, or coming from further afield, there are several straightforward ways to reach the island. The key is knowing what works best for your route, travel style, and budget.

Let's walk through the main options and what to expect from each.

Flying into Palma – The Most Common Route

The vast majority of international travelers arrive in Palma by air. Palma de Mallorca Airport (PMI), also known as Son Sant Joan Airport, is the third-largest airport in Spain and one of the busiest during the summer months. It's located just five miles east of Palma's city center, making transfers quick and relatively painless.

Airline Options:

Palma's airport serves over 180 destinations during peak season, with direct flights from dozens of countries across Europe and a few select cities outside the continent. You'll find regular service from major carriers like Iberia, Lufthansa, British Airways,

Air France, and KLM, as well as a large number of budget airlines—think Ryanair, EasyJet, Vueling, Jet2, and Eurowings. These low-cost carriers offer frequent routes from hubs like London, Berlin, Amsterdam, and Paris, especially between April and October.

Flights from the U.S. and Beyond:

There are currently no direct commercial flights from the United States to Palma, but it's still relatively easy to reach. Most travelers connect through major European airports such as Madrid-Barajas, Barcelona-El Prat, Frankfurt, or London Heathrow. If you're coming from outside Europe, aim to fly into one of those hubs and transfer to a short-haul flight to PMI.

Seasonal Considerations:

During the summer, flights to Palma are plentiful and often inexpensive if booked early. But once the high season tapers off—around late October—flight availability drops, especially from smaller cities. Winter connections still exist, but they're fewer and sometimes require layovers, even from within Spain.

Flying from Mainland Spain

If you're already traveling within Spain—maybe you've been enjoying Barcelona, Madrid, Valencia, or Seville—it's often easiest to hop on a short domestic flight. Flights from these cities to Palma generally take under 90 minutes.

Airlines like Iberia, Vueling, and Air Europa offer frequent departures from:

- Barcelona (about 50 minutes)
- Madrid (about 1 hour 15 minutes)
- Valencia (just under an hour)

Because flights are so short and competitive, prices are usually reasonable, even on relatively short notice.

Taking the Ferry – A Slower but Scenic Option

If you're not in a rush and prefer the slower pace of sea travel, a ferry to Palma can be a unique and surprisingly practical alternative. Ferries operate regularly between the Balearic Islands and the Spanish mainland, especially from Barcelona, Valencia, and Dénia.

Main ferry routes to Palma:

- Barcelona to Palma: about 6.5 to 8 hours (overnight and day sailings)
- Valencia to Palma: around 7 to 9 hours
- Dénia to Palma: about 5.5 to 7 hours (less frequent)

The two major ferry companies on these routes are Baleària and Trasmed. Both offer a range of fares—from simple deck tickets to cabins with beds for overnight trips. Vehicles are allowed on board, which is convenient if you're road-tripping through Spain.

What to Expect on Board:
Most modern ferries are large and well-equipped, with lounges, cafes, and even small shops. You can walk around, stretch your legs, grab a snack, or relax in a reserved seat. Cabins are typically clean and comfortable, making overnight travel a solid choice if you want to save on a hotel.

Which is Better—Flying or Ferry?

There's no one-size-fits-all answer here. If speed and convenience are your top priorities, flying wins hands down. But if you like a bit of adventure, enjoy the open sea, or are traveling with a car, the ferry has its charm.

Choose a flight if:

- You're on a tight schedule
- You're traveling from outside Spain
- You want the most efficient route into Palma

Choose a ferry if:

- You're exploring Spain by car
- You're traveling from Barcelona or Valencia
- You enjoy a slower, more scenic route

Arriving at Palma de Mallorca Airport (PMI)

The airport itself is modern, well-organized, and tourist-friendly. It has four terminals, though most international and domestic flights arrive at Terminals A or C. Signage is clear, and English is widely spoken.

Getting to the city center:
From the airport, it takes about 15–20 minutes to reach central Palma by car or taxi. There are a few ways to make that final leg of the journey:

- **Taxi:** Available directly outside the arrivals area. Metered rates are standard, and the fare into Palma usually ranges from €15 to €25 depending on time of day and traffic.
- **Bus:** EMT's Line A1 runs between the airport and central Palma every 15–30 minutes. It's cheap, reliable, and takes about 25–30 minutes.
- **Car rental:** If you're planning to explore the rest of Mallorca, renting a car directly at the airport is a smart move. Several international and local rental companies have desks onsite.

Tips for Booking Travel to Palma

- **Book early in peak season:** July and August flights fill quickly and prices can spike. Book at least 2–3 months in advance if you're traveling during those months.
- **Travel light if flying budget:** Budget airlines often lure with cheap fares, but baggage fees can add up fast. Always check the luggage policy before booking.
- **Check ferry weather policies:** Ferries are reliable, but rough seas can lead to delays, especially in winter. If you're prone to motion sickness, be prepared.
- **Factor in island time:** Whether flying or sailing, always add some buffer time between your arrival in Palma and any tight schedules. Things move slower here, especially in summer.

In Summary

Getting to Palma de Mallorca is refreshingly uncomplicated. Flights are fast and frequent, ferries are scenic and flexible, and the airport is just minutes from downtown. Whether you're landing by plane or stepping off a ferry, you're only a short ride away from golden beaches, cobbled lanes, and fresh seafood under the Mediterranean sun.

2.3 Transportation Within the City

Once you've arrived in Palma de Mallorca, getting around the city is surprisingly easy—and it doesn't take long to get the hang of it. Despite being the capital of the Balearic Islands, Palma is a relatively compact city with a walkable historic center, a decent public transit network, and a range of options from rental bikes to ride-hailing services. Whether you're aiming to explore the city's old streets, hit the beach, or take a day trip beyond the city limits, there's a transportation method that fits.

Let's break down all the ways to get around—and what to expect with each.

Getting Around on Foot

For many visitors, walking is the go-to choice, especially in and around the historic center. Palma's old town is a maze of narrow streets, centuries-old buildings, hidden courtyards, and sidewalk cafes—most of which can only be appreciated at a pedestrian's pace.

You'll find most major attractions within a manageable distance:

- The Cathedral (La Seu)
- Royal Palace of La Almudaina
- Paseo del Borne shopping street
- Santa Catalina neighborhood
- Parc de la Mar and waterfront areas

If you're staying downtown or in areas like La Lonja or El Terreno, walking will cover a lot of ground comfortably.

Things to know:

- Bring good walking shoes: cobblestone streets can be hard on your feet.
- Summers can be hot: plan walks early in the morning or in the evening.
- Maps matter: even seasoned travelers can get turned around in Palma's winding alleys. Offline maps or GPS apps help a lot.

Public Buses (EMT Palma)

Palma's public bus system, run by **EMT (Empresa Municipal de Transports)**, is reliable, affordable, and fairly easy to navigate. There are dozens of routes covering the city and nearby beaches, as well as connections to Palma Airport (Line A1) and major points of interest.

Tickets and Fares:

- A single ticket costs around €2.
- You can buy tickets directly from the driver (bring small change).
- Discount cards like the **Tarjeta Ciudadana** are available for longer stays, though mainly aimed at residents.
- If you're just visiting, look into prepaid multi-ride cards at kiosks.

Popular Routes:

- **Line 15 & 25**: Popular for reaching beaches like Playa de Palma and El Arenal.
- **Line 3**: Runs through central areas and neighborhoods like Cala Major.
- **Line 1**: Airport to city center and port.

Buses run frequently during the day, though service slows down at night. Timetables are posted at stops, and EMT has a free app that shows real-time arrivals and route planning.

Taxis

Taxis in Palma are widely available and reasonably priced by European standards. You can hail one on the street, find them at taxi stands near major landmarks, or call for a pickup. Most drivers speak at least basic English, and meters are always used (by law).

Rates:

- Initial fare: around €3.50
- Per kilometer: €1.10 to €1.30 (day vs night rates)
- Airport surcharge: typically around €2–3
- A ride from the airport to central Palma usually runs between €15 and €25.

You can also use taxi apps like **TaxiClick** or **Free Now**, which are convenient during busy hours or in less central areas.

Tipping? Not expected, but rounding up is appreciated.

Ride-Hailing and Car Services

Ride-hailing apps aren't as dominant here as in other major cities, but you do have options. Uber doesn't operate in Palma as of now, but **Bolt** and **Free Now** are growing in popularity.

For premium or private rides, companies like **Radio Taxi Palma** and **Palma Transfers** offer pre-booked services, airport pickups, or even full-day car-and-driver packages.

Bicycles and Electric Scooters

Palma is increasingly bike- and scooter-friendly, especially along the seafront promenade and in flat areas of the city. If you're comfortable on two wheels, this can be one of the best ways to explore at your own pace.

Bikes:

- Rental shops are scattered around the city, especially near the beach and city center.
- Prices range from €10 to €20 per day.
- Helmets aren't required by law for adults but are a good idea, especially in traffic.

Scooters:

- Electric scooters (e-scooters) are available through companies like **Acciona** and **Yego**.
- You'll need to download the app, scan the vehicle, and pay per minute.
- Scooter sharing is best for short distances, not long trips.
- Use only on bike lanes or streets—not sidewalks. Helmets are advised.

Renting a Car – Do You Need One?

This really depends on your plans. Within the city, a rental car can be more of a hassle than a help. Parking is limited and expensive, and traffic in the old town can be tight. But if you're planning day trips to the mountains, countryside, or remote beaches, a car gives you the freedom to explore at your own pace.

Where to Rent:

- Major rental companies like Europcar, Hertz, Sixt, and Avis are located at the airport and in the city.
- Prices vary widely depending on season, availability, and vehicle type.
- You'll need a valid driver's license (and an International Driving Permit if yours isn't in Spanish or English).

Parking in Palma:

- Paid street parking is marked with blue lines ("zona azul").
- Underground parking garages are a safer bet but can be pricey.
- Many hotels offer parking but usually charge extra.

Tourist Trains and Hop-On Hop-Off Buses

If you're in town for a short visit or want to get oriented quickly, the red **Hop-On Hop-Off bus** is a solid option. It loops through key areas with an open-top deck, and you can jump off at any stop to explore before catching the next one.

Tickets usually cost around €18–€22 for a 24-hour pass and include headphones with recorded commentary in multiple languages.

There's also a small **tourist train** that runs along some beachfront areas and family-friendly zones—more of a novelty than a main form of transport, but fun for kids or relaxed sightseeing.

In Summary

Palma isn't a city that requires complicated planning when it comes to transportation. If you're staying central, your feet will take you most places. Buses cover the rest affordably, and taxis or scooters fill in the gaps. You can adapt your mode of travel to suit the day—walk the old town in the morning, hop a bus to the beach in the afternoon, and ride a scooter back at sunset.

2.4 Travel Tips and Local Etiquette

Planning a smooth and respectful trip isn't just about knowing where to go—it's also about knowing how to act, what to expect, and how to avoid awkward moments. Palma de Mallorca may be a popular holiday destination, but it's also a city with deep-rooted traditions and a distinct Mediterranean rhythm.

While locals are generally friendly and welcoming, understanding a bit of the culture, pace, and etiquette can go a long way in enhancing your visit.

This section covers practical advice and social customs that every traveler should know before stepping foot on the island.

General Attitude and Social Norms

Palma has a laid-back, coastal vibe that mirrors much of Mediterranean Spain. Life here doesn't move in a rush. Locals tend to value politeness, patience, and a certain level of formality when interacting with strangers. Even in tourist-heavy areas, a bit of courtesy is always appreciated.

- **Greetings matter** – A simple *"Hola"* (hello) or *"Buenos días"* (good morning) when entering a shop or restaurant is basic courtesy.
- **Personal space** – People tend to stand a little closer when chatting, and there's a fair amount of hand movement during conversations.

- **Patience is key** – Things might take longer than expected. It's normal to wait a bit for service or paperwork. Go with the flow.

Language Tips

Spanish (*Castellano*) is the official national language, but don't be surprised if you also hear *Catalan*, or more precisely, the **Mallorquín dialect**, which is widely spoken on the island. That said, in Palma, most people working in tourism speak English—especially in hotels, restaurants, and shops.

Still, learning a few Spanish phrases shows respect and effort:

- *Por favor* – Please
- *Gracias* – Thank you
- *¿Cuánto cuesta?* – How much does it cost?
- *La cuenta, por favor* – The check, please
- *Perdón / Disculpe* – Excuse me

While you'll get by just fine with English in tourist zones, try to avoid assuming everyone speaks it fluently. It's always polite to ask: *¿Habla inglés?* (Do you speak English?)

Dining Etiquette

Eating out in Palma is about more than just food—it's an experience. Meals are social, unhurried, and often stretched over hours, especially in the evening.

Key Points:

- **Meal Times Are Later Than You Might Expect**
  - Lunch: 1:30–3:30 PM
  - Dinner: 8:00–10:30 PM (or later)
    Restaurants may not even open until 8 PM.
- **Tipping** isn't mandatory but is appreciated. Round up the bill or leave 5–10% if service was good.
- **Don't rush your meal.** You'll rarely be given the bill unless you ask for it. It's perfectly normal to linger over coffee or dessert for a while.
- **Tapas and raciones:** Tapas are small portions meant for sharing; *raciones* are larger versions of the same dishes. Don't over-order up front—it's common to order a few things, eat, and then add more.

- **Bread and service fees:** Many restaurants bring bread or olives to the table automatically and charge a small fee. You can refuse them if you like, but it's not considered rude to pay for them.

Dress Code and Modesty

Palma is a beach destination, but that doesn't mean anything goes—especially when you're off the sand.

- **Beachwear is for the beach.** Walking through the old town or into shops and restaurants in swimwear or shirtless is frowned upon. In fact, some city areas now fine tourists who wear bikinis or go shirtless outside beach zones.
- **In churches or religious sites**, dress respectfully. Shoulders should be covered, and avoid short shorts or tank tops. The Cathedral of Santa Maria (La Seu) especially enforces this.
- **At night**, locals tend to dress nicely when going out. You don't need to be formal, but beach sandals and tank tops are best left for the daytime.

Safety and Awareness

Palma is considered safe, even at night, but like any major tourist destination, it's wise to stay alert, especially in crowded areas.

- **Pickpocketing** can occur in busy tourist spots or on public transit. Keep your bag closed and your phone secure. Wear backpacks on your front in crowded areas if needed.
- **Avoid scams:** Be cautious of street performers who pressure for tips or "friendship bracelet" vendors who try to tie something on your wrist without asking.
- **Traffic awareness:** Scooters, e-bikes, and cars may not always stop for pedestrians. Cross only at marked crosswalks and keep an eye out when walking through narrow streets.

Shopping Tips

Markets, boutiques, and local shops are part of Palma's charm, but shopping has its own rhythm:

- **Siesta hours** are still observed in many small shops—typically closing around 2 PM and reopening around 5 PM. Large stores stay open throughout.
- **Sunday closures:** Many shops (except tourist shops and restaurants) are closed on Sundays.

- **Haggling** is not part of local culture. Prices are generally fixed in shops and markets.
- **Eco-friendly bags:** Many stores charge a small fee for bags, so bring a reusable one if you plan to shop frequently.

Sundays and Public Holidays

Mallorca observes several public holidays, and the city slows down dramatically on those days. Museums and shops may be closed, and public transport reduced.

Keep an eye out for:

- **Easter Week (Semana Santa)** processions
- **Assumption Day (August 15)**
- **Fiesta de San Sebastián (January 20)**
- **Christmas and New Year's**

These holidays are great times to catch local celebrations but plan ahead for limited services.

Respect for Local Life

Palma might see millions of tourists a year, but it's also home to thousands of people who live and work here year-round. Being mindful of that helps ensure travelers are seen as guests rather than nuisances.

- **Quiet hours** are usually observed between 10 PM and 8 AM in residential areas.
- **Noise in hotels** or Airbnbs can cause complaints, especially in shared apartment buildings.
- **Public drunkenness** is not tolerated in many areas, particularly in places trying to shift away from rowdy tourism.

Photography Etiquette

- It's generally okay to take pictures in public areas and landmarks, but always ask before photographing people, especially in markets or during religious processions.
- Flash photography is discouraged in churches and museums.

- Some art galleries or boutique shops prohibit photos entirely—look for posted signs.

Cultural Considerations

Mallorca has its own identity within Spain. Locals are proud of their **Mallorquín roots**, so acknowledging the island's culture shows respect.

- Try local food, even if you're tempted by international menus.
- Attend a local festival or artisan market.
- Don't refer to the island simply as a "party spot"—there's so much more to it.

Final Thought

A bit of cultural sensitivity and curiosity goes a long way in Palma de Mallorca. Say hello, slow down, dress appropriately, and show respect for both the people and the place. The result? A richer, more enjoyable trip—and a better connection to the heart of the island.

Chapter 3. Top Attractions in Palma

3.1 Bellver Castle (Castell de Bellver)

Location

Carrer de Camilo José Cela, s/n, 07014 Palma, Mallorca, Spain

Bellver Castle is situated about 3 km west of Palma's city center, perched atop a wooded hill at 112 meters above sea level. The site overlooks the Bay of Palma, offering commanding views of the harbor, the sea, and the sprawling city below.

Admission Fees

- **General Admission**: €4
- **Discounted Admission**: €2 for students, seniors (over 65), and residents of Palma (with valid ID)
- **Free Entry**: Every Sunday, and on select public holidays
- **Children under 14**: Free of charge

Tickets are available at the entrance and do not typically require advance purchase unless visiting with a group or during special events.

Official Website

www.castelldebellver.palma.cat
 Visitors can check updated hours, ticketing details, and event schedules through the official site managed by the Palma City Council.

Opening Hours

- **April to September**:
  Tuesday to Saturday: 10:00 AM – 7:00 PM
  Sunday and Holidays: 10:00 AM – 3:00 PM
- **October to March**:
  Tuesday to Saturday: 10:00 AM – 6:00 PM
  Sunday and Holidays: 10:00 AM – 3:00 PM
- Closed on Mondays and public holidays such as January 1, May 1, and December 25.

Key Features

1. Unique Circular Architecture

Bellver Castle is the only large, fully circular Gothic-style castle in Spain and one of the very few in Europe. Built in the early 14th century under the reign of King James II of Mallorca, its architectural style is a masterclass in symmetry and military ingenuity. The castle features a central circular courtyard, surrounded by a two-level arcade, all enclosed within a perfect ring-shaped structure with four imposing towers.

2. Historical Significance

Over the centuries, Bellver has served multiple purposes: a royal residence, a military stronghold, a prison (notably during the Spanish Civil War), and today, a museum. Its walls have witnessed everything from royal banquets to political imprisonment. One of its most notable prisoners was the Catalan writer and philosopher Gaspar Melchor de Jovellanos, whose cell still exists and is marked.

3. Palma History Museum

Within the castle, the **Museu d'Història de la Ciutat (Palma History Museum)** walks visitors through Palma's evolution—from Roman times through Muslim rule, Christian conquest, and modern city development. Exhibits are bilingual (Spanish and Catalan) and include scale models, artifacts, and visual displays that help contextualize the city's layered past.

4. Courtyard and Gothic Hall

The main courtyard is open to the sky, flanked by two levels of Gothic arches. The upper level houses the main rooms and museum halls. The lower level, often cooler and darker, still reflects the utilitarian and defensive function of the castle. Visitors can walk through the Chapel of Saint Mark, the castle kitchens, and several preserved prison cells, each offering a window into the daily life of earlier centuries.

5. Panoramic Views

The castle's location provides some of the best panoramic views in Palma. From the top of the keep (the tallest tower), visitors are treated to a sweeping vista of the city, the port, the Serra de Tramuntana mountains, and the endless blue of the Mediterranean Sea. The view alone is worth the trip and offers ideal conditions for photography.

Visitor Services

- **Restrooms**: Located near the museum entrance
- **Souvenir Shop**: Small selection of books, guides, and locally crafted items
- **Accessibility**: While the courtyard and some lower-level rooms are accessible, the upper galleries and towers involve staircases that may be challenging for visitors with mobility issues
- **Guided Tours**: Available on request for groups; check the website for arrangements
- **Events**: Occasionally hosts classical concerts, local festivals, and art exhibitions during summer months

Description

Visiting Bellver Castle feels like stepping back into a time when Palma was both a fortress and a throne. The moment you cross the stone bridge over the dry moat, you enter a world of strategic design and Gothic elegance. The circular format gives it an otherworldly feel compared to the typical angular castles of Europe. Walking through the arcaded courtyard, hearing your footsteps echo, and gazing up at the towers, you begin to sense the layers of purpose this castle has served.

The museum inside does an excellent job of anchoring the structure in historical context. Each room adds something to the larger story of Palma, offering glimpses of trade, religion, war, and urban transformation. But even if history isn't your primary interest, the aesthetic beauty of the castle—the way sunlight plays off the limestone, the contrast of medieval stonework against blue skies, the silence interrupted only by the occasional sea breeze—makes it an unmissable landmark.

Tips for Visiting

- The **walk from the city center** to the castle takes about 30–40 minutes uphill. Alternatively, take a bus or taxi to avoid the steep climb.
- The castle is surrounded by **Bellver Forest**, one of Palma's largest green spaces. It's ideal for picnics, shaded walks, or taking a break after your visit.
- If you're interested in photography, aim for **early morning or late afternoon** to catch the best lighting and avoid harsh midday sun.
- Combine your visit with **a stop at nearby Genova**, known for its caves and traditional restaurants.

Bellver Castle stands out as more than just a historical site—it's a vantage point, a sanctuary of silence above the city, and a testament to architectural ingenuity. Whether you're a history buff, a view-seeker, or simply curious, it's one of those places where time feels like it pauses just long enough for you to take it all in.

3.2 Royal Palace of La Almudaina (Palacio Real de La Almudaina)

Location

Carrer del Palau Reial, s/n, 07001 Palma, Mallorca, Spain

The palace sits prominently in Palma's historic center, just beside the iconic La Seu Cathedral. Facing the Parc de la Mar and the Mediterranean Sea, it's in one of the most scenic and culturally significant areas of the city.

Admission Fees

- **General Admission**: €7
- **Reduced Admission**: €4 (EU citizens, students with ID, seniors over 65, and groups)
- **Free Admission**: Wednesdays and Sundays from 3:00 PM to closing, for EU citizens and Latin American nationals (with valid documentation)
- **Children under 5**: Free
- Entry is also free on select national holidays

Tickets are available on-site or online through the Patrimonio Nacional website.

Official Website

www.patrimonionacional.es
This is the official site for Spain's Royal Sites, where you can find up-to-date information on schedules, ticketing, guided tours, and visitor rules.

Opening Hours

- **April to September**:
  Tuesday to Sunday: 10:00 AM – 8:00 PM
- **October to March**:
  Tuesday to Sunday: 10:00 AM – 6:00 PM
- Closed on Mondays, January 1, May 1, and December 25.

Key Features

1. Moorish and Gothic Fusion Architecture

The Royal Palace of La Almudaina is a stunning fusion of Islamic and Gothic styles. Originally a Moorish fortress dating back to the 10th century, it was converted into a royal palace by the Crown of Aragon after the Christian reconquest in the 13th century. Its layout still retains strong elements of Islamic architecture, such as horseshoe arches and inner courtyards, while later Gothic additions—like ribbed vaults and stone façades—reflect its Christian royal use.

2. Hall of the King and Queen

The palace includes multiple state rooms and audience chambers, including the **Sala del Tinell**, which was once the official hall used by monarchs to receive guests. The halls are adorned with period furniture, antique Flemish tapestries, and medieval coats of arms. Although much of the original interior has been restored or replicated, the structure maintains a regal yet austere feel befitting its original military function.

3. Chapel of Santa Ana

This 14th-century chapel, built within the palace grounds, is one of the best-preserved Gothic churches in Palma. It remains functional today and features beautiful stained-glass windows, a high vaulted ceiling, and a single nave design. The simplicity of the chapel contrasts with the richness of the palace interiors.

4. Royal Apartments and Courtyards

The public areas open to visitors include royal chambers, a dining hall, the Queen's room, and ceremonial spaces. Most rooms feature restored period furniture and decor that represent life at the palace during different eras. Courtyards like the **Patio del Rey** and **Patio de Armas** offer open-air views of the palace's interior architecture and are ideal spots to pause and reflect.

5. Seaside Views and Defensive Walls

The palace's strategic location allows for panoramic views of Palma's harbor and bay. Visitors can walk along sections of the old fortress walls and imagine the island's days as a Mediterranean military stronghold. From the palace, you can also enjoy a sweeping view of Parc de la Mar and the waterfront promenade.

Visitor Services

- **Multilingual information panels** are located throughout the palace
- **Restrooms** are available near the entrance
- **Gift shop** offers books, prints, and official memorabilia related to the Spanish Royal Sites
- **Security checks** are conducted at the entrance—large bags and sharp objects are not permitted
- **Photography** is allowed without flash, but tripods are not permitted
- **Guided Tours**: Available by arrangement and highly recommended for history enthusiasts

Description

Walking into the Royal Palace of La Almudaina feels like stepping into a living timeline of Mallorca's ruling dynasties. This palace has stood witness to an incredible mix of cultural legacies—from its origins as an Islamic alcázar to its current function as an official residence for the Spanish royal family when visiting Mallorca. While the royal family now mostly uses Marivent Palace, La Almudaina still holds formal functions and ceremonies on occasion.

The contrast between the medieval stone exterior and the richly appointed Gothic halls is striking. Inside, the subdued lighting, ornate tapestries, and quiet atmosphere evoke a solemn elegance. Each room you walk into tells a different story—whether it's of Moorish emirates, Christian kings, or the modern monarchy.

The tranquil courtyards and sea breezes make the site feel more like a serene retreat than a former fortress, yet its thick walls and strategic hilltop location remind you that this was once a critical piece of Palma's defense.

For travelers who enjoy history, architecture, and quiet reflection, La Almudaina offers a meaningful visit without the crowds typically found at La Seu Cathedral next door.

Tips for Visiting

- **Pair your visit with La Seu Cathedral**, which is right next door. A combined visit makes for a strong half-day itinerary in the city center.
- **Go in the late afternoon** if visiting during warmer months; the lighting is softer, and the interior feels cooler.
- **Wear comfortable shoes**—the stone floors and stairs can be hard on your feet over time.
- **Use the visitor map** provided at the entrance to follow a logical route through the palace and avoid missing key rooms.
- **Don't rush**—even though it's not a massive building, the details in the tapestries, arches, and woodwork are worth lingering over.

The Royal Palace of La Almudaina stands as a silent sentinel of Palma's layered past, gracefully blending two powerful cultural legacies into one unforgettable landmark. It's not just a tourist site—it's a narrative in stone, built by generations of rulers who saw the value of beauty and strength in equal measure.

3.3 Palma Old Town (Casco Antiguo)

Location

The Old Town of Palma is located at the heart of the city, stretching inland from the waterfront and La Seu Cathedral. Bounded roughly by Avinguda d'Antoni Maura to the south and Carrer de la Rambla to the north, this district forms the historical and architectural soul of Palma.

You don't need an exact address—just wander. It's a neighborhood best explored on foot, allowing yourself to get a little lost in its maze of winding streets, hidden courtyards, and sun-washed squares.

Admission Fee

No ticket required. Palma's Old Town is entirely walkable and open to the public year-round, with free access to most of its streets, plazas, and architectural features. Entry fees may apply to specific buildings (such as museums or private courtyards open during special events).

Opening Hours

As a residential and commercial area, the Old Town is always open. Shops, cafes, and attractions typically follow standard Spanish hours:

- **Shops**: 10:00 AM – 1:30 PM and 4:30 PM – 8:00 PM
- **Restaurants and cafés**: Open from noon until late
- **Museums and galleries**: Typically 10:00 AM – 6:00 PM, closed Mondays

Key Features

1. Labyrinthine Medieval Streets

Palma's Old Town feels like a living museum, with its cobblestone lanes and medieval alleyways that twist and fold into each other.

Many of these streets haven't changed in centuries. They're narrow, often shaded, and occasionally open up into charming little squares that catch the breeze and sunlight.

You'll stumble upon everything from 17th-century mansions with wrought-iron balconies to centuries-old churches tucked behind unassuming facades. The quiet here can feel almost surreal, especially early in the morning or during siesta.

2. Historic Mansions and Patios

One of the most defining features of Palma's Old Town is its aristocratic legacy, reflected in the **"casals"**—former noble residences. Many of these historic homes date back to the 15th to 18th centuries and are centered around internal courtyards known as **"patios."**

While most are private, some open their doors to the public during events like the "Patios de Palma" festival in spring. These courtyards are beautifully maintained, featuring arches, columns, fountains, and climbing ivy—each one a quiet oasis tucked behind a heavy wooden door.

3. Jewish Quarter (Call Jueu)

Tucked within the Old Town is the former Jewish Quarter, known as **Call Jueu**. This area is historically significant, dating back to the 13th century, before the expulsion of Jews from Spain in 1492. The street layout remains intact, and you'll find signs pointing out important sites, including where synagogues once stood.

While little remains of the physical structures, the history is deeply woven into the stones. It's a somber yet vital part of Palma's past that adds depth to the city's story.

4. Plaça Major & Surrounding Squares

At the core of the Old Town's Plaça **Major**, the city's main square, known for its symmetrical buildings with yellow façades and green shutters. The square hosts artisan markets, live performers, and seasonal festivals throughout the year. Cafés line the perimeter, making it a lively spot to stop for a cortado or glass of local wine.

From there, narrow pedestrian lanes lead to smaller squares such as **Plaça de Cort**, home to Palma's City Hall and its iconic thousand-year-old olive tree, and **Plaça Santa Eulàlia**, anchored by a striking Gothic church of the same name.

5. Boutique Shops and Artisan Studios

Palma's Old Town is not just about historic sights—it's also one of the best places in Mallorca for boutique shopping. Tucked between centuries-old buildings are independent designers, ceramics workshops, leather artisans, and vintage bookstores.

Local brands selling handmade goods—espadrilles, ceramics, jewelry—give visitors a chance to take home something unique. Stores here close for a few hours in the afternoon, so plan for a relaxed pace and embrace the Mediterranean rhythm.

Visitor Services

- **Tourist Information Points** are located around Plaça Major and La Seu
- **Public restrooms** are available near major plazas and attractions
- **Cafés, bakeries, and tapas bars** are scattered throughout the district
- **Walking tours** (guided or self-guided) are highly recommended and available in multiple languages
- **ATMs and currency exchange kiosks** can be found throughout the area
- **Wheelchair access** can be limited on some cobbled streets, though main squares are navigable

Description

Palma's Old Town is a sensory journey. The scent of orange blossoms drifts from behind iron gates. The sound of church bells echoes from unseen towers. The light shifts dramatically as you weave through shaded corridors that open unexpectedly onto vibrant squares. This is not just an architectural space—it's a mood, a rhythm, a glimpse into how life has flowed through Palma for centuries.

Every corner reveals layers of history: Arab influences in the layout, Gothic spires peeking above the rooftops, Renaissance flourishes on balcony rails. Even the worn steps and weathered walls tell stories.

Yet, it's not frozen in time. Palma's Old Town is lived-in, full of locals chatting in cafés, shopkeepers arranging displays, and artists sketching quietly in sunlit corners. You'll likely pass grandmothers carrying baskets of groceries and students navigating cobbled streets on scooters.

This is the kind of place where no guidebook can cover everything—because the true beauty is in the unexpected. Take a wrong turn. Wander. Sit in a square and just watch. You don't need a plan to enjoy the Old Town—you just need a sense of curiosity.

Tips for Visiting

- **Wear sturdy shoes**—the cobblestones can be uneven and slippery when wet

- **Early mornings and late afternoons** are best for quiet strolls and soft lighting for photography
- **Avoid trying to drive** in the Old Town unless absolutely necessary; the streets are narrow and parking is scarce
- **Bring a bottle of water** and take breaks—there's always a bench or café just around the corner
- **If you're visiting in summer**, consider exploring during the evening hours when the heat subsides and the lights give the Old Town a magical glow

3.4 Es Baluard Museum of Modern & Contemporary Art

Location

Plaça de la Porta de Santa Catalina 10, 07012 Palma, Mallorca, Spain
Just a short walk from the Paseo Marítimo and the Santa Catalina neighborhood, the museum is perched atop Palma's historic city walls, offering one of the most striking views of the bay and marina.

Admission Fee

- General Admission: €6

- Reduced Admission (students, seniors, etc.): €4.50
- Free Admission: Fridays (from 5:00 PM to 8:00 PM), and the first Sunday of each month
- Children under 12: Free

  Prices are subject to change for special exhibitions.

Opening Hours

- Tuesday to Saturday: 10:00 AM – 8:00 PM
- Sunday: 10:00 AM – 3:00 PM
- Closed Mondays and major public holidays

Website

https://www.esbaluard.org

The website provides up-to-date information on current exhibitions, guided tours, workshops, and ticketing options.

Description

Es Baluard isn't just a museum—it's a statement. It's where Mallorca's ancient military past and forward-thinking creative energy collide. Opened in 2004, this modern art museum is housed within the renovated bastion of Sant Pere, part of Palma's original Renaissance-era city walls. The architecture alone is worth the visit: clean lines and minimalist spaces contrast with weathered stone and panoramic views over the sea and city.

The museum's name, "Es Baluard," translates to "The Bastion," a fitting nod to the building's origins as a defensive structure. Today, though, it defends creative freedom. Its collection leans heavily toward Spanish and Mediterranean artists of the 20th and 21st centuries—think Miró, Barceló, Picasso, and Tàpies—alongside international heavyweights like Rebecca Horn, Bill Viola, and Andy Warhol.

The setting adds depth to the experience. Inside, bright galleries and fluid floor plans allow for immersive installations and multimedia exhibits. Outside, terraces and walkways surround the museum, offering sweeping views of the Bay of Palma, the cathedral, and the marina—some of the best in the city.

Key Features

1. Permanent Collection

The museum holds more than 800 works of art, with a focus on modern and contemporary pieces from artists with ties to the Balearic Islands. Regular rotations showcase:

- **Sculptures by Joan Miró**, who spent his final years living and working in Mallorca
- **Large-format works by Miquel Barceló**, known for his organic textures and experimentation
- **Pieces by Pablo Picasso**, offering insight into his lesser-known ceramics
- **Avant-garde installations and kinetic art**, including video, sound, and light-based media

2. Temporary Exhibitions

Es Baluard is known for its ever-changing lineup of exhibitions, often featuring bold, boundary-pushing art. Expect photography, digital media, environmental installations, and politically charged conceptual pieces. Recent shows have spotlighted everything from climate change and feminism to urban decay and digital identity.

These exhibits keep the museum feeling fresh—no two visits are alike.

3. Architecture & Outdoor Spaces

A major draw is the structure itself. The museum's design blends contemporary lines with historical masonry. Walkways curve around the old walls, and many galleries offer natural light and high ceilings, creating a sense of spaciousness.

Don't miss the **rooftop terrace** and the **lower bastion level**, which offer panoramic city views and unique perspectives of Palma's skyline. It's one of the best selfie spots in town—without the tourist crush.

4. Cultural Programming & Events

Es Baluard doubles as a cultural hub. It regularly hosts:

- Art talks and panel discussions with featured artists
- Film screenings and performance art
- Workshops for kids and adults
- Special events during **Nit de l'Art** (Palma's annual art night)
  If you're in town during an exhibition opening, pop in—it's usually lively, open to the public, and includes a glass of local wine.

Visitor Services

- **Audio Guides** available in multiple languages
- **Guided Tours** offered in Spanish, Catalan, and English (book in advance)
- **Museum Shop** selling design books, artist merchandise, and local art
- **Es Baluard Restaurant & Café** serves Mediterranean fusion cuisine with stunning views—ideal for a lunch break or evening cocktails
- **Wheelchair Access** throughout the museum, with elevators and ramps
- **Free Wi-Fi** available in most public spaces
- **Lockers** for bags and coats at the entrance
- **Public Restrooms** on each level

Insider Tips

- Go in the late afternoon, especially on Fridays, to enjoy **free entry** and watch the sun begin to set over the bay. The golden-hour glow on the cathedral and marina is unforgettable.
- The café is underrated—grab a seat on the terrace and just linger. Locals often come here just for coffee and the view.
- While the museum is best known for its visual art, its **interdisciplinary events** are what set it apart—check the website for upcoming talks or performances.
- Bring your camera or phone—but note that flash photography is prohibited inside the galleries.

Why It's Worth Your Time

Es Baluard is more than a place to see modern art—it's where the old and the new sit shoulder to shoulder in conversation. Whether you're a seasoned art lover or just curious, the museum provides a space to slow down, look closely, and reflect. Add to that its scenic location and thoughtfully designed layout, and it becomes one of the most memorable stops in Palma.

For a city so rich in Gothic cathedrals and Moorish relics, this contemporary gem adds a fresh layer to the narrative. If you want to understand not just what Palma was, but what it's becoming—Es Baluard is essential.

3.5 Playa de Palma & the City Beaches

Location

Stretching along the southern coast of Palma from Ca'n Pastilla to El Arenal, Playa de Palma is roughly 4.5 kilometers from the city center. Easily accessible via bus, taxi, or bike, this coastal stretch runs parallel to the Paseo Marítimo, with beach promenades, palm-lined walkways, and seaside cafés that extend into the neighborhoods of Les Meravelles and S'Arenal.

Admission Fee

Public beaches in Palma are free to access.
Optional rentals (approximate rates):

- Sun loungers: €5–€7 per day
- Umbrellas: €5–€7 per day
- Paddle Boats, kayaks, and SUP boards: €10–€20/hour
  Beach clubs and private loungers may charge extra.

Opening Hours

There are no official opening hours, as Playa de Palma is open to the public year-round. Lifeguards are typically on duty from mid-morning to early evening during high season (May–October).

Overview

Playa de Palma isn't just a single beach—it's a vibrant coastal strip that captures the sun-soaked energy of Mallorca's capital. Stretching for nearly six kilometers, it offers an expansive escape for beachgoers of every kind: families, solo travelers, party lovers, and those who simply want to unwind under the Mediterranean sun.

The beach is broad and clean, with soft golden sand and warm, shallow waters that are ideal for swimming. Dotted along the promenade are open-air cafés, chilled-out beach bars, water sports kiosks, souvenir stands, and bike rental shops. It's the kind of place where you can grab a mojito, rent a paddleboard, or simply people-watch for hours on end.

What's most notable is its versatility. Mornings are peaceful, great for joggers and early swimmers. Afternoons fill with sunbathers and families. By dusk, the boardwalk pulses with music and conversation as beach bars light up and the nightlife crowd trickles in.

Key Features

1. Expansive Sandy Shores

Playa de Palma boasts a long, wide stretch of fine, golden sand—perfect for laying out a towel, building sandcastles, or taking long barefoot walks. The shoreline is gently sloped, making it family-friendly and safe for kids to swim. The beach is divided into sections by numbered "balnearios" (beach bars), which help you navigate and choose your vibe—whether it's relaxed and quiet or lively and social.

2. Calm Waters and Water Sports

The clear, turquoise water stays relatively shallow for several meters out, making it safe for casual swimmers. You'll often see locals doing laps parallel to the shore. If you're up for some adventure, vendors offer:

- Jet ski rentals
- Banana boat rides
- Parasailing
- Stand-up paddleboarding (SUP)

- Windsurfing and kitesurfing, especially on breezy afternoons

Water activities are generally available from April through October.

3. Seaside Promenade

A wide pedestrian walkway runs along the beach, perfect for a leisurely stroll or a morning bike ride. It's lined with palm trees, restaurants, beach clubs, and shops, and there's no shortage of benches to stop and admire the view. In the evenings, the promenade comes alive with street musicians, roller skaters, and outdoor diners.

4. Beach Clubs and Dining

From casual beach bars serving tapas and cocktails to trendy clubs like **Purobeach** and **Anima Beach**, there are plenty of ways to indulge. You can sip sangria while lounging on a shaded daybed, grab fresh seafood with sea views, or find a family-friendly restaurant with paella and ice cream on the menu.

5. Family-Friendly Zones

Parts of Playa de Palma are especially geared toward families. Lifeguard towers are posted at regular intervals, and some stretches have playgrounds and safe bathing areas. Many local restaurants offer kid-friendly menus and shaded terraces.

6. Accessibility and Facilities

The beach is fully equipped with modern amenities:

- Showers and changing stations
- Public restrooms
- Lifeguard stations during peak months
- Wheelchair ramps and beach-accessible pathways in designated areas
- Bike racks and scooter parking along the promenade

Visitor Services

- **Lifeguards**: On duty daily during the summer season
- **Rental Services**: Parasols, loungers, lockers, and water gear available onsite
- **Bike Rentals**: Available along the promenade for €10–€15/day
- **Shops**: Souvenirs, sunscreen, beachwear, and cold drinks
- **ATMs**: Found along the promenade in convenient locations
- **Security Patrols**: Regular presence to ensure safety during the day and evening

Insider Tips

- Head to **Balneario 6** if you're in the mood for a party scene. For quieter stretches, try the sections closer to Ca'n Pastilla.
- Want an unforgettable sunrise? Visit just after dawn—you'll share the beach with joggers and early risers, and the pink skies over the water are absolutely worth waking up for.
- Sundays can get very crowded, especially in high summer, so consider visiting midweek if you prefer a calmer scene.
- Keep an eye on the **flag system** near lifeguard posts. Green means it's safe to swim, yellow means caution, and red means no swimming.
- Bring your own towel and umbrella if you're on a budget—the rental fees add up over multiple days.

Why It's Worth Your Time

Whether you're looking for a quick dip between sightseeing stops or a full day of seaside lounging, Playa de Palma delivers. It's close enough to the heart of the city for easy access but long enough to feel like its own destination. You can spend a quiet afternoon reading in the sand, join a volleyball game, hit the waves, or dance barefoot at a sunset beach party. And when the sun finally sinks below the horizon, Palma's beaches don't fall silent—they shift into a more relaxed, twilight rhythm that continues well into the night.

In short, Playa de Palma is a microcosm of Palma itself: vibrant, diverse, and always inviting.

3.6 Arab Baths (Banys Àrabs)

Location

Carrer de Can Serra, 7, 07001 Palma, Mallorca, Spain
Nestled within Palma's Old Town, just a few minutes' walk from the Cathedral (La Seu) and the Royal Palace of La Almudaina. Access is through a small garden behind the Church of Sant Francesc.

Admission Fee

- General Admission: €3–€4 per person (cash only)
- Children under 12: Free
- No guided tours, but informational plaques are available on-site.

Opening Hours

- Daily: 9:30 AM – 6:00 PM
- Open year-round (except major holidays)

Note: Hours may vary slightly by season; mornings are typically less crowded.

Website

There is no official website for the Arab Baths. For current information, it's best to check updated listings through Palma's tourism board or via local heritage organizations.

Overview

Tucked away in a quiet courtyard surrounded by lush greenery, the **Arab Baths (Banys Àrabs)** are one of the few remaining examples of Islamic architecture in Palma. These modest but evocative ruins are all that's left of what was once a luxurious hammam during the Moorish occupation of Mallorca. Though compact in size, the space transports visitors back nearly a thousand years into the island's layered past.

Walking into the main chamber—marked by its squat dome and signature horseshoe arches—feels like stepping into another world. The room's thick stone walls, soft natural light, and silence are a stark contrast to the buzz of modern Palma just outside. For history lovers and curious wanderers alike, the Arab Baths offer a rare window into the Balearic Islands' Islamic period, which stretched from the 10th to the 13th century.

Key Features

1. Central Domed Room

The most iconic space in the complex is the **tepidarium**, or warm room. It's built in a circular layout topped with a low, domed ceiling pierced by twelve small star-shaped openings that let in shafts of light. Twelve columns—each believed to be reused Roman or Byzantine pieces—support the dome, giving the chamber a timeless, almost mystical appearance. This room was used for warm bathing, relaxation, and socializing.

2. Caldarium and Frigidarium (Now in Ruins)

While the main room is well-preserved, the adjoining **hot** (caldarium) and **cold** (frigidarium) rooms have mostly crumbled, though traces of their layout are still visible. You can see remnants of the heating system, including an old furnace and the hypocaust—a subfloor chamber where hot air circulated to heat the floors and walls.

3. Serene Garden Courtyard

One of the real hidden gems is the garden surrounding the baths. It's quiet, shaded, and full of flowering plants, cacti, and orange trees. Benches are scattered throughout, offering a peaceful place to sit and reflect after your visit. The garden itself feels like a little oasis—cool, calm, and beautifully maintained.

4. Architectural Significance

The Arab Baths are thought to have been part of a nobleman's private residence rather than a public bathhouse. They date back to the 10th or 11th century, built during the Almoravid or Almohad reigns, showcasing a style that blends Islamic, Roman, and even Visigothic elements. The use of recycled columns, as well as the detailed brickwork and dome structure, reveal a lot about the resourcefulness and aesthetics of that era.

Visitor Services

- **Information Boards**: Multilingual panels provide brief descriptions of the site's history and layout.
- **Garden Seating**: Benches available for rest and quiet reflection.
- **No restrooms or café** on site; public facilities are nearby in the Old Town.
- **Photography** allowed (no flash inside the domed chamber).
- **No guided tours**, though some local walking tours include this site on their route.

Insider Tips

- This is a **short visit**—you'll only need about 15–30 minutes to explore the site and gardens, but it's worth lingering to soak in the atmosphere.
- Early mornings or late afternoons are the best times to go, especially during summer when the garden is shaded and the space is quieter.
- Combine your visit with a walking tour of the **Old Jewish Quarter**—the Arab Baths are just around the corner.
- Bring **cash** for the entry fee; credit cards are not accepted.
- It's not wheelchair accessible due to narrow entrances and uneven stone flooring.

Why It's Worth Your Time

While not a large-scale attraction, the Arab Baths hold deep cultural and historical value. They're among the oldest structures in Palma still standing, quietly revealing the influence of Islamic rule on the island's architecture and daily life. What they lack in size, they make up for in atmosphere—the quiet, the filtered light through the dome, the gentle buzz of bees in the garden—it's all deeply grounding.

For those who appreciate history, architecture, or peaceful spots away from the crowds, the Arab Baths are a simple but unforgettable stop on your Palma itinerary.

Chapter 4. Neighborhoods and Districts

4.1 Old Town (Casco Antiguo)

The **Old Town of Palma**, known locally as *Casco Antiguo*, is the historic core of the city—and arguably its most atmospheric and culturally rich area. With narrow medieval lanes, ancient stone buildings, sun-dappled plazas, and a layered architectural timeline that dates back over a thousand years, the Old Town offers an intimate look at Palma's past while continuing to pulse with present-day life.

Located just inland from the bay and surrounding La Seu Cathedral, this district is compact and walkable, but incredibly dense with history, charm, and detail. Every street seems to carry its own story, from quiet corners with tiled religious shrines to grand palaces hiding behind heavy wooden doors.

Architectural Identity

Palma's Old Town showcases an eclectic mix of **Gothic, Baroque, Moorish, and Modernist** architecture. Buildings here often feature arched stone entryways, grand wooden shutters, and shaded inner courtyards—called *patios*—which are often hidden from the street but visible through wrought iron gates. These patios were once the heart of Mallorcan noble homes, and their preservation offers insight into aristocratic life from centuries past.

You'll also find 13th-century churches tucked beside 19th-century townhouses, alongside revamped apartments and boutique hotels occupying what were once noble estates or merchant houses. These elegant facades and alleyways have been immaculately preserved, thanks to strong local heritage protection efforts.

Main Landmarks and Streets

The Old Town is home to several of Palma's most important landmarks and cultural sites:

- **La Seu Cathedral** – The dramatic Gothic cathedral that dominates the skyline, especially striking when viewed from the Parc de la Mar.
- **Royal Palace of La Almudaina** – Just next to the cathedral, this historic palace blends Moorish and Gothic styles and has served as a royal residence for centuries.
- **Plaça Major** – A lively central square framed by yellow-painted buildings, arcades, and outdoor cafés. It serves as the beating heart of the district and is a popular gathering spot.
- **Carrer de Sant Miquel** – A lively shopping street lined with boutiques, galleries, and cafés, running north from Plaça Major.
- **Carrer de Jaume II and Carrer de Colom** – These narrow lanes are great for wandering, full of artisan shops and small tapas bars.
- **Jewish Quarter (Call Jueu)** – Tucked behind the main thoroughfares, this lesser-known section offers quiet alleyways and historical markers related to the once-thriving Jewish population of medieval Palma.

Cultural Vibe

Casco Antiguo feels like a living museum but without the stiffness. It's a place where residents still hang laundry from tiny balconies, where antique stores sit across from trendy concept cafés, and where street musicians provide an ever-present soundtrack. The pace here is slower, more reflective, and best enjoyed on foot.

What makes the Old Town particularly inviting is its ability to balance authenticity with contemporary appeal. You'll stumble upon ancient bakeries using recipes passed down for generations, then find yourself drawn into a sleek boutique or design-forward wine bar just a few doors down.

Dining and Nightlife

The district is packed with **family-owned restaurants**, modern eateries, and **traditional tapas bars**. You'll find Mallorcan classics like *sobrasada*, , and *ensaimadas* alongside international cuisine in both casual and upscale settings.

For nightlife, the Old Town leans toward a relaxed, intimate atmosphere. Think cozy wine bars, rooftop lounges with cathedral views, and underground jazz venues. It's a place for conversation and culture rather than wild party scenes.

Shopping

Shopping in Casco Antiguo focuses on **local craftsmanship and small boutiques**. Expect to find leather goods, hand-painted ceramics, woven textiles, antique books, handmade jewelry, and gourmet food shops selling local olive oil, wines, and island-made sweets.

Markets are also a draw, with **Mercat de l'Olivar** (just on the fringe of the Old Town) offering a colorful display of seafood, produce, and local specialties.

Accommodation Options

Many travelers choose to base themselves in the Old Town due to its historic ambiance and proximity to key sights. Accommodation here ranges from **boutique hotels** in centuries-old mansions to **luxury townhouses**, and **stylish apartments** tucked behind ancient facades. Properties like Hotel Mamá, Can Bordoy, and Sant Francesc Hotel Singular are notable examples offering world-class amenities with heritage flair.

Getting Around

The area is pedestrian-friendly and **not suitable for driving**, with many streets closed to cars or too narrow for anything but scooters. Expect to do a lot of walking, but the rewards are plenty—getting lost is half the charm. If you need to go further out, taxis and buses are accessible from the outer edges of the district.

Who Will Love It

The Old Town is perfect for:

- Travelers who appreciate **architecture, art, and history**
- Couples seeking a **romantic escape** in charming, walkable surroundings
- Food lovers looking to sample **authentic Mallorcan cuisine**
- Photographers chasing **natural light, color, and texture**

Local Tips

- **Early mornings and evenings** offer the most tranquil atmosphere, especially in peak season.
- Don't be afraid to wander—**the smaller the street, the bigger the surprises**.
- Look up: many of the best architectural details—balconies, carvings, and ironwork—are above eye level.
- Stop for a coffee or *café con leche* at a street-side table and simply watch the city go by.

Final Thoughts

Palma's Old Town is more than just the city's historical heart—it's where Palma's identity truly comes to life. Every stone and street tells a story, from Moorish foundations to medieval churches to modern flair. It's a place to slow down, take in the details, and let the city's layers unfold around you. Whether it's your first visit or your fifth, Casco Antiguo always feels fresh—and utterly timeless.

4.2 Santa Catalina

Just west of Palma's Old Town, across the tree-lined **Avinguda Argentina**, lies **Santa Catalina**—one of the city's most dynamic and colorful neighborhoods. Once a quiet fishing village on the edge of the capital, Santa Catalina has transformed into Palma's bohemian heartbeat, known for its artistic edge, international flair, and a buzzing food and nightlife scene that draws locals and visitors alike.

This district blends old-world charm with a fresh, creative energy that's hard to resist. Think brightly painted façades, vintage storefronts, potted plants on every balcony, and a casual, unhurried atmosphere. If the Old Town is steeped in tradition, Santa Catalina is where tradition gets a modern twist.

History & Character

Santa Catalina's roots date back to the **19th century**, when it developed as a **fishing and maritime neighborhood** near Palma's port. Many of its original houses were modest one- or two-story buildings designed to house seafarers and laborers. Over time, it retained a strong working-class vibe even as the city grew around it.

Fast forward to the early 2000s, and Santa Catalina started to attract a wave of **artists, chefs, and creative entrepreneurs**, drawn by its affordability, character, and great location. Since then, it has evolved into a cosmopolitan enclave while keeping its laid-back personality intact.

Santa Catalina Market (Mercat de Santa Catalina)

At the neighborhood's core is the **Santa Catalina Market**, one of Palma's most beloved food markets and a staple of daily life in the area. This is no tourist gimmick—it's where chefs, residents, and foodies stock up on local produce, seafood, meats, cheeses, and fresh bread.

The market also features **a number of stalls where you can sit down and enjoy tapas, oysters, sushi, or even gourmet burgers**, all freshly prepared using ingredients sourced just steps away. It's lively in the mornings and packed by lunchtime, especially on weekends.

Dining Scene

Santa Catalina is often called **Palma's culinary capital**, and for good reason. You'll find everything from traditional Mallorcan taverns and Spanish tapas bars to Nordic-inspired bakeries, vegan cafés, Middle Eastern restaurants, Peruvian cevicherías, and fine-dining fusion spots.

It's not unusual to stumble across a low-key bistro serving Michelin-level dishes without the pomp. Many chefs here source directly from the neighborhood market, so freshness is practically guaranteed.

Popular spots include:

- **Patrón Lunares** – a former fisherman's club turned lively, nautical-themed restaurant
- **Vandal** – creative small plates with global influences
- **Santosha** – cozy and health-forward, run by expats with a passion for organic food

Nightlife and Social Scene

Santa Catalina doesn't shut down when the sun goes down. It's one of Palma's **top nightlife destinations**, particularly for those who prefer laid-back drinks over clubbing.

The area is packed with:

- **Cocktail lounges**
- **Craft beer bars**
- **Wine taverns**
- **Live music venues**

You'll find both locals winding down after work and travelers starting their evenings. The crowd is diverse—young professionals, artists, entrepreneurs, and plenty of international residents. There's a palpable sense of community here that blends effortlessly with its trendiness.

Shops and Boutiques

While not a primary shopping district like Passeig des Born, Santa Catalina is dotted with **independent shops and concept stores**. You'll come across vintage clothing boutiques, handmade jewelry shops, indie bookstores, and quirky home décor spots. It's ideal for finding unique gifts or a new favorite piece of art or apparel.

Architecture and Street Life

Santa Catalina has a distinct look compared to other Palma neighborhoods. Expect:

- Narrow one-way streets
- Colorful townhouses with traditional **Mallorcan shutters**
- Open **balconies lined with plants and laundry lines**
- Minimal car traffic
- A friendly, dog-walking, bike-riding vibe

Some buildings still show their modest maritime roots, while others have been renovated with modern touches—but none feel out of place.

There's also a noticeable **Scandinavian and Northern European influence**, as many residents and business owners hail from Sweden, Germany, the UK, and the Netherlands. This blend gives the neighborhood a worldly feel, even though it's authentically local at its core.

Accommodation Options

Santa Catalina offers a range of accommodations, from boutique hotels to high-end vacation rentals and modern apartments. While it lacks the large luxury hotels found along the waterfront, what it does have is personality.

Many visitors opt to stay in:

- Boutique guesthouses with historic charm
- Stylish with rooftop terraces
- Designer flats perfect for longer stays

Staying in Santa Catalina means **walking distance to the market, the port, and the Old Town**, but with a quieter, more residential feel.

Best For

Santa Catalina appeals to:

- Foodies and culinary travelers
- Digital nomads and creatives
- Couples and solo travelers
- Visitors seeking a local lifestyle with city access

Insider Tips

- **Visit the market before 1 p.m.** for the freshest goods and best energy.
- Dinner starts late—**many restaurants don't open before 7:30 or 8 p.m.**
- Take your time strolling around—the best finds are often behind unassuming doors.
- For a great sunset, **head toward the waterfront near Es Jonquet**, just south of the neighborhood.

Final Thoughts

Santa Catalina is more than just a trendy neighborhood—it's the kind of place where life unfolds slowly and vibrantly. It's where coffee is sipped rather than gulped, where meals are shared not rushed, and where every corner seems to have a bit of personality. If you want to see Palma through the eyes of someone who lives here, even if just for a few days, Santa Catalina is where you should start.

4.3 El Molinar and Portixol

Tucked just east of Palma's city center, **El Molinar and Portixol** form a seamless stretch of coastal charm that perfectly blends traditional fishing roots with contemporary Mediterranean lifestyle. What once were humble fisherman's quarters has blossomed into one of the most desirable and picturesque areas in the entire Bay of

Palma. These neighborhoods have a relaxed, seaside vibe, a strong local identity, and are ideal for travelers seeking a quieter, more scenic slice of city life.

Overview and Atmosphere

El Molinar and Portixol—often referred to together due to their close proximity—sit right along the seafront promenade, about a 20–30 minute walk from Palma's historic core. The promenade, known locally as the **Passeig Marítim**, stretches for several kilometers and is popular with joggers, dog walkers, cyclists, and families enjoying the breeze.

This area is **less about landmarks and more about lifestyle**. Life here revolves around the sea—mornings start with locals sipping coffee at a beachfront café, afternoons are spent strolling or lounging along the sand, and evenings often include fresh seafood and sundown drinks with uninterrupted views of the Mediterranean.

El Molinar: A Traditional Touch

El Molinar retains more of its traditional, local flavor. It's quieter and more residential, with whitewashed homes, tiled roofs, and narrow back streets lined with palm trees. The name "Molinar" comes from the old windmills ("molins") that once dotted the landscape—some of which can still be spotted around the neighborhood.

The pace here is slow and soothing. You'll see elderly residents chatting from balconies, fishermen tending to their boats, and kids cycling to the bakery around the corner. While there's been a recent influx of investment and renovation, El Molinar has held tightly to its original character.

Portixol: Trendy by the Sea

Just next door, **Portixol** is where the scene livens up a bit. It's become something of a hotspot for both locals and international visitors, thanks to its **hip beach cafés, boutique bars, and stylish apartments**. Once a quiet fishing harbor, Portixol's marina now welcomes sleek yachts and paddleboards, all against the backdrop of a postcard-perfect promenade.

It's not flashy or commercial—just effortlessly cool. Think **renovated sea-facing townhouses**, art galleries, rooftop terraces, and a casual-but-upscale food scene. On weekends, it fills with a relaxed mix of Mallorcans, expats, and travelers all enjoying the views and sea breeze.

Dining and Café Culture

El Molinar and Portixol are **a haven for food lovers**, especially those who enjoy long, leisurely meals by the water. The culinary offerings here lean heavily toward seafood, Spanish classics, and global fusion—with plenty of fresh, local ingredients.

Some notable restaurants and cafés include:

- **Es Vaixell** – an unpretentious seafood joint with top-tier paella
- **Portixol Hotel Restaurant** – refined Mediterranean cuisine in an elegant setting
- **Tast Club Portixol** – contemporary tapas with a creative flair
- **The Coco** – a laid-back café popular for brunch, craft cocktails, and ocean views

Most eateries offer **terrace seating** just steps from the water, and dining here is less about speed and more about savoring the moment.

Beaches and Recreation

There are **small, clean urban beaches** scattered along this stretch of coastline, many with calm, shallow waters that are perfect for swimming. While these aren't the wide, resort-style beaches found elsewhere on the island, they're charming, accessible, and far less crowded than Palma's busier Playa de Palma.

The **beachfront promenade** is the area's main attraction for many. It connects Portixol and El Molinar to Palma in one direction and continues on to Ciutat Jardí and beyond in the other. Whether you're up for a run, a scenic bike ride, or just a breezy evening walk, this is one of the best spots to stretch your legs by the water.

Rental shops along the promenade offer:

- **Bicycles and e-scooters**
- **Stand-up paddleboards**
- **Kayaks**
- **Rollerblades**

Accommodation

There's a growing number of accommodations in these neighborhoods, ranging from **boutique hotels and guesthouses to vacation rentals and modern serviced apartments**. Because of the limited space and preservation of low-rise architecture, don't expect high-rise resorts—this is where charm outweighs scale.

Notable places to stay:

- **Portixol Hotel & Restaurant** – a chic boutique hotel with a rooftop terrace and sea views
- **Apartments and Airbnbs** – ideal for longer stays, many with beach access and self-catering amenities

Staying here offers a **quiet alternative to the city center** with easy access to Palma by foot, bike, or taxi.

Getting There and Around

From Palma's Old Town, El Molinar and Portixol are reachable by:

- **Walking or biking** along the promenade (20–30 minutes)
- **Public bus** (lines 15 and 25 serve the area regularly)
- **Taxi or rideshare** (under 10 minutes)

The neighborhoods are compact and walkable—once you're here, **you won't need a car**.

Who It's For

These areas are perfect for:

- Couples seeking a romantic seaside escape
- Families looking for quiet, safe surroundings
- Solo travelers who want an authentic local vibe
- Food lovers who prefer oceanfront meals and laid-back cafés

It's also a top pick for those staying longer on the island—digital nomads and part-time residents are increasingly drawn to this peaceful yet connected part of Palma.

Local Tips

- **Sunsets are spectacular** from the Portixol harbor wall—arrive early for the best spot.
- Many restaurants fill quickly—**make reservations**, especially on weekends.
- Early mornings here are magical. If you're up with the sun, you'll get the promenade almost to yourself.

Final Thoughts

El Molinar and Portixol strike a rare balance: seaside serenity with the cultural buzz of a city close by. You'll get the charm of a fishing village, the amenities of a boutique district, and the joy of daily life unfolding against a Mediterranean backdrop. For visitors who want more than just a hotel stay—for those who want to live like a local, even for a few days—this is the place to be.

4.4 La Lonja and Paseo Marítimo

The districts of **La Lonja** and **Paseo Marítimo** together offer a dynamic mix of Palma's historical elegance and its modern, energetic spirit. Though adjacent, these two neighborhoods contrast in character:

La Lonja is rooted in Gothic architecture and old-world charm, while Paseo Marítimo stretches along the waterfront, pulsing with nightlife, luxury yachts, and the steady rhythm of the sea. Whether you're exploring during the day or soaking up the electric buzz after sundown, this area offers a compelling combination of culture, leisure, and beauty.

La Lonja: A Walk Through History

La Lonja (also spelled "Llotja") is a small but culturally rich quarter located just west of Palma's Old Town. The district is named after its architectural gem, **La Lonja de Palma**, a 15th-century maritime trade exchange that showcases the city's medieval mercantile past.

The area is made up of **narrow, cobbled lanes**, historic stone facades, and beautifully restored mansions. It's quieter during the day—ideal for unhurried walks and hidden courtyards—and livelier in the evening, as its tapas bars and wine cellars begin to fill.

Highlights of La Lonja:

- **La Lonja de Palma (Sa Llotja)** – This emblematic Gothic building was once the center of maritime commerce. It's open to the public and hosts rotating exhibitions.
- **Art galleries and studios** – The area is known for its small, independent art spaces.
- **Tapas culture** – La Lonja is one of Palma's best spots to bar-hop through cozy taverns and try local favorites like "pa amb oli" or "pimientos de padrón."

Despite its compact size, La Lonja radiates atmosphere. It's a great place to linger over a glass of local wine or explore the quieter, more intimate side of Palma's historic core.

Paseo Marítimo: The City's Coastal Strip

Stretching along the seafront just south of La Lonja, the **Paseo Marítimo** (officially called Avenida Gabriel Roca) is a long, palm-lined boulevard that follows Palma's marina and leads all the way past the city toward the beachside districts. It's a scenic artery that connects the **Port of Palma** with the city's nightlife and yachting scene.

The promenade is flanked by:

- **Luxury yachts and cruise ships** docked in the harbor
- **Trendy cafés and cocktail bars**
- **Upscale hotels and modern apartment blocks**
- **Nightclubs and lounges** that come alive after dark

It's not just for partygoers, though. During the day, the **waterfront path is popular with walkers, runners, and cyclists** enjoying the sea breeze and panoramic views of the cathedral and bay.

Dining, Nightlife, and Entertainment

Together, La Lonja and Paseo Marítimo offer **some of the best dining and entertainment options** in Palma:

In La Lonja:

- **La Bóveda** – Classic tapas with a loyal following.

- **Ribello** – A stylish Italian spot in a historic building.
- **Abaco** – An unforgettable cocktail bar housed in a 17th-century palace, adorned with flowers, fruits, and candlelight.

Along Paseo Marítimo:

- **Mar de Nudos** – Modern Mediterranean cuisine with sea views and a high-end vibe.
- **Restaurante Pesquero** – Known for seafood and sunsets over the port.
- **Social Club Mallorca** – A sleek bar/lounge with DJs and rooftop views of the marina.

When the sun sets, the Paseo becomes a social hub. While La Lonja retains its intimate charm, Paseo Marítimo takes on a livelier personality with popular clubs like **Tito's** (temporarily closed for redevelopment but historically a Palma institution) and newer venues catering to all music tastes.

Places to Stay

This area has a range of accommodations, many with **sea views and walking access to both the old town and marina**. It's ideal for visitors who want to be close to the action without being in the middle of tourist crowds.

Top choices include:

- **Hotel Mirador** – Boutique hotel with harbor views and a rooftop pool.
- **Hotel Costa Azul** – Bright, modern rooms facing the bay.
- **Hotel Saratoga** – A four-star stay near both La Lonja and the Paseo, known for its jazz club and rooftop terrace.

The area is also a favorite among cruise passengers due to its proximity to the **Port of Palma**.

Getting Around

Both La Lonja and Paseo Marítimo are centrally located and easy to navigate:

- **Walking** is the best way to explore both neighborhoods. La Lonja is very walkable and best discovered on foot.
- **Buses and taxis** are readily available along the Paseo.
- **Bike lanes** stretch along the waterfront, and bike rental shops are plentiful.

From this area, you can easily reach Palma Cathedral, the Old Town, Bellver Castle, or even hop on a ferry for a day trip.

Local Tips

- **La Lonja is busiest after 7 PM**, especially for dining—arrive early or book ahead.
- While Paseo Marítimo is lively at night, **early mornings here are peaceful**, perfect for sunrises over the harbor.
- Dress smart-casual in the evening—this area leans a bit more upscale, especially in restaurants and bars.
- Some of the clubs have **seasonal hours**, with many events in spring and summer.

Who Should Visit This Area?

- Travelers interested in **Palma's nightlife and culinary scene**
- Visitors who enjoy **art, architecture, and urban history**
- Couples and groups seeking **romantic dinners, stylish hotels, and marina views**
- Anyone arriving by **cruise ship** or looking to stay near the harbor

Final Thoughts

La Lonja and Paseo Marítimo offer a snapshot of Palma's many layers: from centuries-old Gothic halls and art-filled alleys to sleek yachts and buzzing terraces. The contrast is what makes this area so compelling. Whether you're after a quiet wine bar in a cobbled courtyard or a front-row seat to Palma's vibrant nightlife, this district gives you the best of both worlds—history and horizon, past and present.

Chapter 5. Where to Stay

5.1 Luxury Hotels and Boutique Stays

Palma de Mallorca is home to a refined collection of upscale accommodations that balance architectural charm, top-tier hospitality, and exclusive amenities. Whether you're drawn to converted palaces, contemporary design sanctuaries, or intimate adults-only escapes, the city offers several standout properties. Below are some of the most distinguished luxury hotels and boutique stays in Palma, ideal for travelers who appreciate comfort, detail, and elevated service.

Sant Francesc Hotel Singular

Address: Plaça de Sant Francesc 5, 07001 Palma, Mallorca
Price Range: Approximately €400–€500+ per night
Contact: +34 971 710 505 · info@santfrancesc.com
Website: www.hotelsantfrancesc.com

Location and Setting:

Located in the heart of Palma's historic Old Town, Sant Francesc Hotel Singular sits on a quiet square opposite the gothic Sant Francesc Basilica. The hotel occupies a restored 19th-century mansion that elegantly combines historic architecture with modern refinement. Its position places guests within walking distance of the cathedral, city walls, and local boutiques.

Key Features:

Sant Francesc offers 42 rooms and suites, each uniquely designed with a mix of original frescoes, wooden beams, and curated artwork. Rooms include high-end bedding, Nespresso machines, rain showers, and luxury bathroom products. The rooftop terrace features a plunge pool with panoramic views across Palma's rooftops and spires, including La Seu Cathedral. The hotel's Quadrat Restaurant & Garden delivers modern Mediterranean dishes using seasonal and local ingredients, while the Lobby Bar and courtyard provide stylish spaces to relax with a drink.

Visitor Services:

Guests can enjoy a wellness area equipped with a small gym, massage treatment rooms, and a sauna. The 24-hour reception and concierge desk assist with tour bookings, restaurant reservations, and special requests. Additional services include valet parking, complimentary Wi-Fi, daily housekeeping, in-room dining, and airport transfers upon request.

Concepció by Nobis

Address: Carrer de la Concepció 34, 07012 Palma, Mallorca
Price Range: €350–€450+ per night
Contact: +34 971 915 025 · info@concepciohotels.com
Website: www.concepciobynobis.com

Location and Setting:

Positioned between Palma's Old Town and the vibrant Santa Catalina district, Concepció by Nobis brings together Swedish minimalism and Mallorcan heritage. The hotel is housed in a 16th-century former soap factory that has been reimagined by award-winning Scandinavian designers. Its central location allows easy access to both historic sites and trendy cafes.

Key Features:

The hotel offers 31 guest rooms with a calm and curated aesthetic. Interiors feature exposed beams, natural stone, wood furnishings, and soft textiles in muted tones. Many rooms overlook the peaceful inner courtyard or surrounding rooftops. The hotel's rooftop terrace offers a tranquil space with a plunge pool, and the on-site restaurant

Xalest specializes in creative Mediterranean small plates. The communal spaces are airy, understated, and ideal for quiet reading or a relaxed drink.

Visitor Services:
Concepció by Nobis provides wellness offerings such as massage services, yoga sessions, and a small fitness area. Concierge support includes tour and transport arrangements, local insights, and in-room amenities tailored to personal preferences.

The staff maintain high service standards while preserving a warm and relaxed atmosphere. The hotel also offers bicycle rentals, room service, and daily housekeeping.

El Llorenç Parc de la Mar

Address: Plaça Llorenç Villalonga 4, 07003 Palma, Mallorca
Price Range: €300–€400+ per night
Contact: +34 971 714 747 · info@elllorenc.com
Website: www.elllorenc.com

Location and Setting:
Located beneath the imposing La Seu Cathedral and overlooking Parc de la Mar, El Llorenç offers a quieter alternative to the city center's buzz. It's an adults-only hotel designed for those seeking peace, indulgence, and architectural elegance. Its Moorish-inspired aesthetic mixes with minimalist Swedish design to create a warm and atmospheric interior.

Key Features:
This luxury property features 33 rooms and suites, each offering plush beds, rainfall showers, mood lighting, and bespoke touches. The rooftop level is one of the most scenic in Palma, with a long infinity pool that overlooks the bay and historic skyline. Dining is a highlight here. Santi Taura, a renowned local chef, runs the hotel's culinary program, including a Michelin-guided restaurant offering tasting menus built around traditional Mallorcan flavors and seasonal ingredients.

Visitor Services:
El Llorenç offers an extensive wellness area, which includes a fitness center, treatment rooms, Jacuzzi, and a Finnish sauna. Guests can take advantage of personalized concierge services, 24-hour front desk support, in-room dining, airport transfers, valet parking, and complimentary Wi-Fi. The ambiance is particularly well-suited to couples and solo travelers seeking serenity and fine dining.

These hotels represent the best of Palma's hospitality scene, where thoughtful design, heritage preservation, and a focus on guest comfort come together. Each offers a distinct atmosphere, but all are consistently praised for attentive service, aesthetic detail, and top-tier amenities.

5.2 Mid-Range and Family-Friendly Options

Traveling to Palma de Mallorca doesn't have to stretch your budget thin—especially if you're looking for a place that balances comfort, location, and family-friendly amenities. From charming local hotels with traditional flair to contemporary stays near the beach, Palma offers a wide range of mid-tier options that cater to couples, families with kids, and small groups. Here are some standout choices in this category that are well-regarded for their atmosphere, cleanliness, service, and convenience.

Hotel HM Balanguera

Address: Carrer Balanguera 37, 07011 Palma, Mallorca
Contact: +34 971 456 152
Website: www.hmhotels.net

Location and Overview:

Just a 15-minute walk from the heart of Palma's Old Town, Hotel HM Balanguera offers a clean, modern stay with strong Mallorcan influences. Its whitewashed walls, handcrafted wooden elements, and Mediterranean design make it a relaxing urban retreat for travelers seeking a break from the city's more crowded zones.

Ideal For: Couples, small families, and solo travelers who want access to both the city center and nearby beaches without paying top-tier prices.

Key Features:

The hotel has 40 rooms with minimalist, island-inspired decor. While it's not a full resort, it offers thoughtful touches like private balconies, flat-screen TVs, comfortable beds, and rainfall showers. The rooftop terrace includes a small plunge pool and seating area that's especially inviting in the evenings.

Family Services:

Though the hotel doesn't have dedicated play areas or kids' programming, it's quiet atmosphere and spacious rooms make it a comfortable choice for families with older children. Cribs are available on request, and nearby restaurants are family-friendly.

Visitor Services:

Breakfast is available daily, and the lobby lounge serves light snacks and drinks. The staff are helpful and multilingual, offering assistance with tour bookings, taxis, and directions. Wi-Fi is free throughout the property.

Hotel Isla Mallorca & Spa

Address: Carrer de Pilar Juncosa 7, 07014 Palma, Mallorca
Contact: +34 971 281 200
Website: www.islamallorca.com

Location and Overview:

Set just off the Paseo Marítimo promenade, this 4-star hotel is a popular option for those wanting to be close to both the marina and Palma's cultural attractions. The nearby Bellver Forest also makes it a good base for morning walks or jogs.

Ideal For: Families, couples, and travelers seeking value without sacrificing comfort.

Key Features:

This hotel offers over 150 rooms ranging from standard doubles to spacious suites and apartments. Rooms are contemporary with large windows, and many have balconies with views of the harbor or city. The in-house wellness center includes a full spa with massage treatments, a sauna, and a small gym. There's also an outdoor pool surrounded by sunbeds.

Family Services:
Family rooms and interconnected units are available, and the breakfast buffet includes child-friendly options. While there isn't a full kids' club, the staff are accommodating and happy to help with baby cots, high chairs, and nearby recommendations for family dining or entertainment.

Visitor Services:
The hotel has an on-site restaurant and bar, 24-hour reception, private parking (for a fee), bike rentals, laundry service, and complimentary Wi-Fi. It's a reliable and practical option for longer stays, especially for guests planning to explore by rental car.

Hotel Abelux

Address: Carrer del 31 de Desembre 31, 07004 Palma, Mallorca
Contact: +34 971 751 256
Website: www.hotelabelux.com

Location and Overview:
Situated just north of Palma's city center, Hotel Abelux is an affordable and well-maintained hotel with quick access to the main train and bus stations. It's a simple stay, but it earns solid reviews for cleanliness and customer service.

Ideal For: Budget-conscious families, small groups, or independent travelers who want convenience.

Key Features:
Rooms are straightforward but include essentials like air conditioning, free Wi-Fi, desks, and modern bathrooms. While it doesn't have on-site dining, there are plenty of cafes, bakeries, and casual restaurants nearby.

Family Services:
Abelux has triple and quadruple rooms that work well for families. Staff are helpful with arranging taxis and giving suggestions for family outings, such as the Palma Aquarium or the beach.

Visitor Services:

There's a continental breakfast option served each morning, a 24-hour front desk, luggage storage, and rental car arrangements available directly through the hotel. While it's not luxurious, it's a solid base for travelers who want to save on lodging and spend more on activities.

Brick Palma

Address: Carrer de la Ferreria 14, 07002 Palma, Mallorca
Contact: +34 971 595 821
Website: www.brickpalma.com

Location and Overview:

Tucked into a quiet street near Palma's Old Town, Brick Palma is a creative and artsy hotel with a focus on sustainability and local flair. With cozy rooms and an inviting communal vibe, it's especially popular with young families and travelers who enjoy a slightly alternative experience.

Ideal For: Budget-minded couples, families with teens, and digital nomads.

Key Features:

Rooms come in a variety of layouts, including lofts and family suites with bunk beds. The decor is simple and playful, featuring exposed brick walls and handmade furniture. The hotel includes a co-working area, a casual breakfast cafe, and an outdoor terrace. It's a favorite among long-weekenders and international guests looking for a home base with character.

Family Services:

The hotel is child-friendly without being geared entirely toward families. Rooms are spacious, and larger groups will find the suite options ideal. Board games, coloring kits, and extra towels are available on request.

Visitor Services:

Free Wi-Fi, luggage storage, bike rentals, and tourist information are available at reception. It's a relaxed stay with a strong local feel—less formal, but warm and welcoming.

Each of these hotels reflects a different flavor of Palma, from urban chic to beach-adjacent and artistic hideouts. They provide an excellent compromise between affordability and comfort, while also giving you easy access to the island's top attractions. Whether you're traveling with kids, friends, or just want something low-key and dependable, these mid-range options give you the essentials—without skipping the charm.

5.3 Budget-Friendly Hotels and Hostels

Palma de Mallorca might have its share of glamorous resorts and boutique hotels, but it also welcomes travelers who prefer to keep things simple, affordable, and down-to-earth. Whether you're a solo backpacker, a couple looking for value, or a group traveling on a tight budget, there are plenty of great places to stay that offer comfort, convenience, and character—without the hefty price tag.

These budget accommodations are all well-rated for cleanliness, safety, and service. They may not come with marble bathrooms or rooftop pools, but they do offer the essentials—and in many cases, a unique local vibe that pricier places can't replicate.

The Boc Hostels – Palma Albergue Juvenil

Address: Carrer d'Aragó 8, 07005 Palma, Mallorca
Contact: +34 871 577 108
Website: www.bochostels.com

Overview:
This trendy, modern hostel is one of the best options in the city for travelers looking to stay somewhere stylish on a tight budget. The interiors are sleek and minimalist, with pops of bright color and a youthful atmosphere. It caters mainly to younger travelers, solo adventurers, and groups of friends, but mature travelers who enjoy a relaxed social setting are also welcome.

Location:
Located near Plaza España and the Intermodal Station, The Boc is within walking distance of Palma's Old Town, shopping streets, and plenty of restaurants and bars.

Key Features:
Guests can choose between dorm-style rooms with bunk beds or private rooms with en-suite bathrooms. There's a shared kitchen, a lounge with games and books, and even a small pool and rooftop terrace. The overall vibe is social, but not rowdy.

Visitor Services:
Free Wi-Fi, laundry facilities, luggage storage, air conditioning, and bike rentals are all available. Staff are friendly and knowledgeable about the area, always ready with local tips and bus schedules.

Urban Hostel Palma

Address: Carrer de Joan Miró 5, 07014 Palma, Mallorca
Contact: +34 971 282 634
Website: www.urbanhostelpalma.com

Overview:
This small hostel is located in a traditional Mallorcan house and offers a more local and homey feel. It's not a party hostel, making it an excellent choice for travelers who want to meet others without sacrificing their sleep.

Location:
Set in the Santa Catalina neighborhood, the hostel is just a short walk from the marina, Bellver Castle, and some of the best tapas bars in Palma.

Key Features:
Urban Hostel Palma features mixed and female-only dorms, as well as a few private rooms. The shared kitchen and common areas are simple but functional, and the building's original character has been well preserved.

Visitor Services:
There's free Wi-Fi throughout, personal lockers, laundry service, and a relaxed check-in process. Guests appreciate the quiet atmosphere and the helpful staff who can point out nearby sights or help arrange day trips.

Hostal Regina

Address: Calle San Miguel 77, 07002 Palma, Mallorca
Contact: +34 971 716 513
Website: www.hostalreginapalma.com

Overview:
For travelers who prefer a hotel-style experience but still want to stick to a budget, Hostal Regina is a solid pick. It's basic, but clean and centrally located—perfect for those who plan to spend most of their time out exploring rather than lounging in their room.

Location:
Right in the middle of Palma's commercial district and just a few minutes' walk from Plaza Mayor, the hostel is perfectly positioned for sightseeing, shopping, and public transport access.

Key Features:

All rooms come with private bathrooms, flat-screen TVs, fans, and comfortable beds. While there's no on-site dining, cafés and bakeries are just steps away.

Visitor Services:

Wi-Fi is included, as well as daily room cleaning. The reception staff are friendly, and there's an easy luggage drop-off option for those arriving early or departing late.

Apuntadores 8

Address: Carrer Apuntadors 8, 07012 Palma, Mallorca
Contact: +34 971 713 491
Website: www.apuntadores8.com

Overview:

This no-frills guesthouse in the historic La Lonja district is an excellent base for those who want to stay central without spending a fortune. It's housed in a charming old building and offers great views over the city from its rooftop terrace.

Location:

You couldn't ask for a better location—just a stone's throw from the Cathedral, the harbor, and some of the best restaurants and bars in Palma.

Key Features:

Rooms are compact but functional. Some have en-suite bathrooms, while others share facilities. The rooftop terrace is a standout feature, especially at sunset.

Visitor Services:

Free Wi-Fi, friendly reception, and luggage storage are available. While breakfast isn't served on-site, there are numerous cafes within a minute's walk.

Hostal Bonany

Address: Carrer de Almirante Cervera 5, 07014 Palma, Mallorca
Contact: +34 971 737 924
Website: www.hostalbonany.com

Overview:

This family-run guesthouse offers quiet, affordable lodging in a residential part of Palma. It's simple, clean, and very welcoming—ideal for couples, solo travelers, and those who appreciate a more relaxed pace.

Location:
Located near Bellver Castle and the Paseo Marítimo promenade, it's close enough to the action while still being a quiet retreat after a long day of sightseeing.

Key Features:
Rooms are basic but comfortable, with private bathrooms, fans or air conditioning, and flat-screen TVs. Many rooms come with a balcony. There's also a small garden and a pool, which is rare for a property in this price range.

Visitor Services:
Free Wi-Fi, a communal kitchen, bicycle parking, and a vending machine for drinks and snacks. The staff are helpful and go out of their way to ensure guests feel at home.

These budget-friendly accommodations provide a great way to enjoy Palma without draining your wallet. While amenities are generally simpler, the convenience of location, cleanliness, and the warm welcome you'll receive at these spots can easily outweigh the luxury extras you'd pay for elsewhere. Whether you want the sociable energy of a hostel or the simplicity of a guesthouse, Palma offers plenty of options for every kind of thrifty traveler.

5.4 Best Areas to Stay for Different Travelers

Palma isn't a massive city, but it's full of personality—and each neighborhood has its own distinct feel. Whether you're here for beaches, nightlife, culture, or just some peace and quiet, knowing where to stay can shape your entire trip. To help narrow things down, here's a breakdown of the best areas to consider based on what kind of traveler you are.

For First-Time Visitors: Old Town (Casco Antiguo)

Why it works:
This is Palma's historic heart and an excellent base for travelers who want to see the main sights without wasting time on public transport.

You'll be within walking distance of the Cathedral, Royal Palace, Arab Baths, and countless shops and cafes tucked into charming stone alleyways.

What to expect:
Narrow, winding streets, a mix of Gothic and Moorish architecture, and that unmistakable old-world charm. It's a great spot for aimless wandering, discovering hidden courtyards, and soaking up local culture.

Ideal for:
First-timers, history buffs, romantic getaways, and travelers who love being in the center of it all.

For Foodies and Night Owls: Santa Catalina

Why it works:
This hip, lively neighborhood is known for its buzzing restaurant scene, cocktail bars, and international vibe. It feels a bit like a Mediterranean version of Brooklyn or Shoreditch—laid-back but full of energy.

What to expect:
Trendy cafes, tapas bars, fusion restaurants, and one of the city's best markets—Mercat de Santa Catalina. It's a great place to stay if you're looking to eat your way through Palma and still be close to major attractions.

Ideal for:
Couples, solo travelers, digital nomads, and anyone who enjoys a vibrant local scene with plenty of places to eat, drink, and hang out.

For Beach Lovers: Playa de Palma and El Arenal

Why it works:
If sand, sun, and a sea breeze are high on your list, Playa de Palma is the area to book. Stretching several kilometers along the coast, it's lined with beachfront hotels, bars, and bike paths. El Arenal, at the far end, is a bit livelier and tends to attract a younger, more party-oriented crowd.

What to expect:
Long sandy beaches, beach clubs, laid-back resorts, and an easygoing vibe. It's farther from the city center, but public buses and bike rentals make getting into town simple enough.

Ideal for:
Families, beachgoers, group travelers, and budget-conscious vacationers who prefer to be close to the coast.

For a Local, Quiet Stay: El Molinar and Portixol

Why it works:
These former fishing villages have turned into Palma's relaxed, seaside gems. With their wide promenades, quiet beaches, and local eateries, they offer a slower pace without being too far from the action.

What to expect:
Harbor views, casual cafes, bike paths, and fewer crowds. These areas are great for those who want to live more like a local and enjoy quiet mornings and scenic walks along the waterfront.

Ideal for:
Couples, long-stay visitors, families with young kids, and anyone seeking tranquility with easy access to the city.

For Luxury and Seclusion: Son Vida

Why it works:
Set in the hills just outside Palma, Son Vida is all about privacy, elegance, and breathtaking views over the bay. This upscale residential area is home to luxury villas, five-star hotels, and golf courses.

What to expect:
Gated communities, resort-level service, and a peaceful escape from the buzz of

downtown. If you're not worried about walking distance and value luxury, this is your spot.

Ideal for:
Luxury travelers, honeymooners, golf lovers, and those seeking a retreat-style stay.

For Budget Travelers and Solo Explorers: Pere Garau

Why it works:
Often overlooked in guidebooks, Pere Garau is one of Palma's more affordable and authentic neighborhoods. It has a multicultural population, a lively local market, and decent public transport connections.

What to expect:
No-frills local life, small family-run eateries, and fewer tourists. It's not postcard-pretty, but it's real, affordable, and safe.

Ideal for:
Solo travelers, backpackers, long-term travelers, and anyone traveling on a budget who doesn't mind staying off the tourist path.

A Quick Recap:

Traveler Type	Best Area	Highlights
First-Timers	Old Town	Historic sights, walking distance to major attractions
Food Lovers & Night Owls	Santa Catalina	Trendy bars, international dining, cool vibe
Beach Seekers	Playa de Palma / El Arenal	Beachfront hotels, nightlife, boardwalk

Couples or Quiet Getaways		El Molinar / Portixol	Seaside walks, calm setting, local cafes
Luxury Stays		Son Vida	Secluded, upscale, golf courses
Budget Travelers		Pere Garau	Affordable, authentic, local flavor

In the end, the best place to stay really depends on what you're hoping to get out of your time in Palma. The good news? With such a compact city layout and easy transport options, no matter where you stay, you're never too far from anything. Whether you want beach mornings, museum afternoons, or lively nights out, Palma has a neighborhood that fits just right.

Chapter 6. Food and Drink Scene

6.1 Traditional Mallorcan Dishes

Mallorcan cuisine isn't just an offshoot of Spanish food—it's its own proud tradition shaped by centuries of Mediterranean influence, local ingredients, and island culture. From ancient agricultural recipes passed down through generations to rustic, soulful cooking tied to religious and seasonal festivals, Mallorcan food offers something earthy and deeply satisfying. In Palma, you'll find it on both white tablecloths and in humble taverns tucked away in the old town.

Let's break down some of the most iconic traditional dishes that define Mallorcan food culture.

1. Ensaimada: The Sweet Spiral Icon

Arguably the most famous Mallorcan dish, the ensaimada is a light, spiral-shaped pastry made with flour, sugar, eggs, and lard (traditionally "saim" in Mallorca Catalan, hence the name). It has a soft, flaky texture and comes in various versions—some dusted with powdered sugar, others filled with cream, custard, or even pumpkin jam (known as *cabello de ángel*).

Locals often eat it with coffee for breakfast or as a mid-morning snack. You'll also find boxed ensaimadas in the airport being hauled home as edible souvenirs by tourists and expats alike.

Where to try it: For authenticity, visit **Forn des Teatre** or **Ca'n Joan de S'Aigo**, a 300-year-old café where the locals go for their sweet fix.

2. Sobrasada: The Spreadable Sausage

Sobrasada is a soft, cured pork sausage seasoned heavily with paprika. It's often spread on rustic bread, used in cooking, or served warm over roasted vegetables. The smoky, slightly spicy flavor comes from local paprika (*tap de corti*) and a slow curing process that happens in the mild, humid air of the island.

You'll see sobrasada on breakfast platters, mixed into stews, and even folded into scrambled eggs or pasta.

Pro tip: Try a slice of rustic bread smeared with sobrasada and a drizzle of honey—simple and unforgettable.

3. Tumbet: Mallorca's Answer to Ratatouille

This traditional vegetable casserole is made with layers of potatoes, eggplant, zucchini, bell peppers, and tomatoes—often topped with garlic or tomato sauce and olive oil. It's typically baked until everything melts together into a warm, comforting medley.

Tumbet is usually served as a side, but it's hearty enough to stand alone as a vegetarian main. Some modern twists include topping it with fish or a fried egg.

Best enjoyed in: Traditional Mallorcan family-run restaurants, especially in summer when vegetables are fresh and local.

4. Frito Mallorquín (Frit Mallorquí)

This is one of the oldest dishes on the island and not one for the faint of heart. Frito Mallorquín is made from offal (usually lamb or pork liver), potatoes, onions, peppers, and peas—all fried with garlic and fennel in olive oil. It's deeply flavorful, slightly earthy, and unapologetically traditional.

Many locals grow up eating this dish, particularly during Easter or major festivals. It speaks to the island's resourceful past, where nothing from an animal went to waste.

Not a fan of offal? Some restaurants serve a fish-based version or a vegetable-only twist.

5. Arroz Brut ("Dirty Rice")

This hearty rice stew gets its name from the way the spices and meat give the broth a rich, murky color. Ingredients can vary by season and cook, but the base usually includes rice, chunks of meat (like rabbit or pork), mushrooms, green beans, and aromatic spices like cinnamon and clove.

Served in a large clay pot, it's warming, deeply savory, and typically eaten in colder months or at family Sunday lunches.

Tip: Order it for two—it's almost always made in large portions.

6. Pa amb Oli (Bread with Olive Oil)

It doesn't get simpler—or more essential—than this. A slice of rustic Mallorcan brown bread (*pa moreno*) is rubbed with garlic and ripe tomato, then drizzled with local olive oil and sprinkled with sea salt. That's the base. From there, toppings vary: local cheese, jamón serrano, anchovies, or sobrasada.

Locals eat it as a snack, starter, or even light dinner. It's available everywhere, from tapas bars to beachside cafes.

Where to get it: Just about anywhere, but try **Bar Bosch** or **Celler Sa Premsa** for a classic take.

7. Coca de Trampó

Think of it as Mallorca's version of pizza—only rectangular and made with a thin pastry base, topped with chopped tomato, onion, and green pepper (*trampó salad*). It's served at room temperature and often eaten as a tapa or snack.

It's especially popular during summer, as it's light and easy to make in large batches.

8. Sopes Mallorquines (Mallorcan Soups)

Despite the name, these "soups" are really thick vegetable stews soaked up by slices of dry country bread. Cabbage, green beans, garlic, onion, and tomato form the base, with seasonal greens or sometimes a bit of meat added in. The bread absorbs the broth, turning it into a dense, spoonable dish perfect for winter.

You won't see this dish often in tourist restaurants—but it's beloved by locals and shows up on traditional menus.

9. Conill amb Ceba (Rabbit with Onion)

This dish combines chunks of rabbit meat with heaps of slowly caramelized onions, garlic, wine, and local herbs. It's tender, sweet-savory, and very much rooted in the island's rural food history.

It's usually served with potatoes or seasonal vegetables, and it's especially popular in the countryside.

10. Local Cheeses and Wines

Mallorca has its own D.O. (Denominación de Origen) for wine and a strong tradition of cheese-making. You'll find semi-cured goat and sheep cheeses like *Formatge de Maó* and local specialties flavored with herbs or paprika.

The wine regions of Binissalem and Pla i Llevant produce crisp whites and bold reds, many from native grapes like Manto Negro or Prensal Blanc.

Don't skip: A wine-and-cheese platter at a countryside bodega or urban wine bar.

Final Thoughts

Eating in Palma isn't just about filling up—it's about connecting with the island's roots. The food is simple in structure but rich in heritage. From humble dishes built on olive oil and garden produce to bold sausages and hearty rice stews, Mallorcan cuisine is a story told in flavor.

So don't just look for what's trending—ask for what's local. Look for the dishes that have fed families for generations. Ask your server for the house special. And always say yes to dessert.

6.2 Best Restaurants and Tapas Bars

Palma de Mallorca offers a rich dining landscape that effortlessly blends rustic tradition with modern flair. Whether you're in the mood for a simple plate of local sobrasada or an artful tasting menu with Mediterranean views, you're in the right city. The food scene is alive with variety, from bustling tapas joints and historic cellers to quiet fine dining establishments tucked into the old town's winding alleys.

Below is a curated list of standout restaurants and tapas bars where you can savor the real flavor of Palma.

1. Ca'n Joan de S'Aigo

Type: Café & Traditional Dessert House
Location: Carrer de Can Sanç, 10, 07001 Palma
Price Range: € – €€
Website: www.canjaumallorca.com

This iconic spot dates back to the 1700s and is arguably Palma's most beloved café. It's best known for ensaimadas and thick hot chocolate, but they also serve savory bites like sandwiches and quiches. The decor feels like a time capsule—wooden beams, marble tables, and waitstaff who've likely worked there for decades.

Don't miss: A classic ensaimada with almond ice cream.

2. Bar España

Type: Tapas Bar
Location: Carrer de Can Escursac, 12, 07001 Palma
Price Range: €€
Website: bar-espana.negocio.site

Bar España is one of Palma's best-known tapas spots—and for good reason. It's cozy, unpretentious, and buzzing with locals. The menu mixes classic Spanish tapas with Mallorcan twists. The atmosphere is relaxed but always energetic, especially in the evenings.

What to try: Croquettes, spicy chorizo, and grilled octopus. Wash it down with a local red.

3. La Rosa Vermutería

Type: Vermouth Bar & Tapas
Location: Carrer de la Rosa, 5, 07003 Palma
Price Range: €€
Website: larosapalma.com

La Rosa is a stylish throwback to old-school vermouth bars, serving artisan vermouths on tap alongside an extensive menu of traditional tapas. The setting is equal parts retro and trendy, with vintage posters and ambient lighting.

Recommended dish: The "ensaladilla rusa" (Spanish potato salad) and Iberian pork cheeks.

4. Marc Fosh

Type: Michelin-Starred Modern Mediterranean
Location: Carrer de la Missió, 7A, 07003 Palma
Price Range: €€€€
Website: marcfosh.com

For a true fine dining experience, Marc Fosh offers creative Mediterranean cuisine using local ingredients in an elegant yet relaxed atmosphere. The Michelin star is well-deserved. The tasting menu is a culinary journey that highlights Mallorca's bounty with modern technique.

Highlights: Expect refined dishes like sea bass with fennel purée or artichoke confit with anchovy emulsion.

Ideal for: Celebrations, anniversaries, or anyone looking to splurge on something unforgettable.

5. Tast Union

Type: Upscale Tapas Bar
Location: Carrer de la Unió, 2, 07001 Palma
Price Range: €€
Website: tast.com

Tast Union is popular with locals and visitors who want quality tapas in a refined, modern setting. It's larger and more polished than some of the casual bars, making it a good option for groups or those new to tapas dining.

Top picks: Duck foie gras with fig jam, grilled prawns, and seafood paella.

6. Celler Sa Premsa

Type: Traditional Mallorcan Restaurant
Location: Plaça del Bisbe Berenguer de Palou, 8, 07003 Palma
Price Range: €€
Website: cellersapremsa.com

A staple in Palma for over 60 years, this large, bustling restaurant captures the essence of old Mallorca. Set in a former wine cellar, with barrels lining the walls and waiters in classic uniforms, it's the kind of place where time slows down and portions are generous.

Must-try: Tumbet, frito mallorquín, and Mallorcan-style roast lamb.

7. Sadrassana Restaurant & Cocteleria

Type: Fine Dining & Cocktail Bar
Location: Plaça de la Drassana, 15, 07012 Palma
Price Range: €€€
Website: sadrassana.com

Set in a beautifully restored 19th-century mansion in La Lonja, this restaurant combines high-end Mallorcan cuisine with an elegant cocktail bar. It also shares space with an art gallery, making it an immersive cultural experience.

Dish to try: Suckling pig with quince or lobster rice.

Great for: Romantic dinners or a stylish night out.

8. El Camino

Type: Modern Tapas Bar
Location: Carrer de Can Brondo, 4, 07001 Palma
Price Range: €€–€€€
Website: elcaminopalma.es

El Camino is a newer entry on the scene but has made waves for its open-kitchen format and high-quality ingredients. Think market-fresh seafood, seasonal vegetables, and well-curated wines, all served over a long marble bar.

Perfect for: Solo diners or couples who want to eat well without committing to a formal setting.

9. Bodega La Rambla

Type: Casual Tapas Bar
Location: La Rambla, 5, 07003 Palma
Price Range: €
Website: Not available

This old-school bodega feels like a time warp in the best possible way. The wine is local, the tapas are simple but hearty, and the atmosphere is pure neighborhood charm. It's a no-frills kind of place where locals read the paper and share olives.

Try: Pa amb oli with anchovies and a glass of house vermouth.

10. Ombu Tapas & Cocktails

Type: Modern Tapas Fusion
Location: Passeig del Born, 5, 07012 Palma
Price Range: €€€
Website: ombupalma.com

Located right on the bustling Passeig del Born, Ombu leans into fusion tapas with flair. You'll find classics like patatas bravas alongside inventive takes like tuna tataki with mango or avocado hummus with paprika chips. The cocktails are also a strong draw.

Good for: Travelers who want something trendy and stylish in a central location.

Final Thoughts

The food scene in Palma doesn't ask you to choose between rustic and refined—it encourages you to enjoy both. Whether you're diving into small plates at a family-run bar in Santa Catalina or splurging on a Michelin-starred menu tucked behind a quiet courtyard, you're tasting more than food. You're getting a bite of the island's history, geography, and soul.

6.3 Local Markets and Street Food

Palma de Mallorca's food culture lives and breathes in its markets. While the city is home to elegant restaurants and polished tapas bars, it's in the local markets and street stalls that you'll find the heartbeat of everyday life. These spaces—bustling, noisy, fragrant—offer everything from fresh seafood to handmade empanadas. Whether you're shopping for a picnic, sampling a local delicacy on the go, or just soaking up the atmosphere, Palma's markets are worth slowing down for.

Here's a closer look at some of the city's most beloved markets and the street food traditions that go with them.

Mercat de l'Olivar

Location: Plaça de l'Olivar, 4, 07002 Palma
Opening Hours: Monday to Saturday, 7:00 AM – 3:00 PM (some food stalls stay open later)
Website: mercatolivar.com

Situated near Plaça d'Espanya in the city center, Mercat de l'Olivar is Palma's largest and most comprehensive food market. It's a bit of everything under one roof—farmers selling seasonal produce, butchers with cured meats hanging overhead, fishmongers laying out today's catch, and tapas bars serving oysters, croquettes, and glasses of white wine to patrons leaning on the counter.

The market is clean, lively, and well-organized. One section is purely for fresh ingredients, while another is dedicated to prepared foods and small restaurants. You can easily lose track of time wandering through the stalls, sampling everything from olives to artisanal cheeses.

What to try while you're there:

- Fresh oysters with lemon and sea salt, eaten standing up
- Iberico ham sliced to order
- Stuffed piquillo peppers or seafood pintxos at one of the on-site bars

It's the kind of place where locals do their daily shopping and visitors come to get a crash course in Mallorcan flavor.

Mercat de Santa Catalina

Location: Plaça Navegació, s/n, 07013 Palma
Opening Hours: Monday to Saturday, 7:00 AM – 5:00 PM
Website: mercatdesantacatalina.com

Santa Catalina, the trendier, bohemian neighborhood west of the Old Town, is home to this smaller but equally beloved market. While Mercat de Santa Catalina still caters to locals shopping for produce and meat, it's also become a bit of a hotspot for foodies and curious travelers.

The energy here is laid-back but vibrant. Colorful fruit displays spill over wooden crates, fishmongers call out the morning's specials, and cozy counters invite you to pull up a stool and order a bite. Because Santa Catalina is a multicultural district, you'll also find international flavors here—sushi rolls, poke bowls, and Vietnamese spring rolls often sit alongside local treats.

Recommended bites:

- Grilled squid with aioli
- Empanadas Mallorquinas (stuffed pastries with peas, lamb, or tuna)
- A glass of vermouth paired with anchovies or pickled olives

On Saturday mornings, it's especially lively, as the weekend crowd mingles over brunch-style plates and local wine.

Pere Garau Market (Mercat de Pere Garau)

Location: Carrer de Pere Garau, 33, 07006 Palma
Opening Hours: Monday to Saturday, 6:00 AM – 2:30 PM (outdoor stalls open earlier)
Website: No official site, but popular with locals

Less polished and more authentic than the other markets, Pere Garau is where you'll find real, working-class Palma. This isn't a market dressed up for tourists—it's raw, energetic, and very much about the everyday. It's also one of the few places in the city where live animals are occasionally sold (mostly poultry), giving it an old-world feel.

What makes it special? The sheer diversity. You'll hear a mix of Mallorcan, Spanish, Arabic, and Chinese being spoken. The food reflects that too—roast pork sandwiches, freshly fried churros, noodles, and spicy grilled meats are just a few of the offerings.

Why go: To feel like a local and sample flavors from both the island and immigrant communities who've made it their home.

Don't miss: The spicy Mallorcan sausage sandwiches (llonganissa picant) and handmade sobrasada rolls.

Street Food & Pop-Up Culture

While Palma doesn't have the same level of street food culture you might find in big Asian or Latin American cities, it does have a growing scene of food trucks, seasonal pop-ups, and festival food stands. Keep an eye out for food trucks that show up near Palma's beaches or at events like Nit de l'Art and Sant Sebastià in January.

You might find:

- Grilled chorizo or morcilla on a baguette
- Bocadillos made with spicy sobrassada and cheese
- Freshly fried calamari served in a paper cone
- Mini paellas cooked over open flames at night markets

The rise of pop-up food events—especially during summer—has brought more fusion cuisine into the mix, from Korean-style fried chicken to Argentine empanadas. The vibe is always casual and perfect for eating on the go.

Farmers' Markets and Artisan Fairs

On weekends, especially in spring and summer, smaller farmers' markets and artisan food fairs appear throughout Palma. Look out for events in the Plaça Major or Parc de la Mar, where local bakers, cheesemakers, and olive oil producers sell their goods. These are great for picking up edible souvenirs—jars of tapenade, honey from local hives, or packets of sea salt harvested from the island's southern shores.

Final Notes

Markets are more than just a place to eat—they're a window into daily life on the island. They capture the rhythm of the city in a way few other places can. Whether you're looking to snack on the go, stock your Airbnb with fresh ingredients, or just soak in the buzz of Palma's food scene, you'll find plenty to love in its markets.

6.4 Wine, Cocktails, and Café Culture

Palma de Mallorca isn't just a beautiful Mediterranean city—it's also a place where people take their drinks seriously. Whether you're sipping a chilled local wine on a sun-drenched terrace, trying a carefully crafted cocktail after dinner, or spending a slow afternoon at a café with a cortado and a pastry, this city has perfected the art of drinking with style, comfort, and purpose.

Here's a closer look at the island's most popular drinks and the best places to enjoy them.

Wine Culture: Local Bottles, Global Flavor

Mallorca's wine scene has grown in both quality and reputation over the last two decades. With warm sun, mineral-rich soil, and centuries of winemaking tradition, the island produces some surprisingly complex wines. Many visitors are caught off guard by just how good the local varieties are—and how affordable, too.

The two main wine regions on the island are **Binissalem** and **Pla i Llevant**, both producing a mix of red and white wines using native grape varieties such as **Manto Negro**, **Callet**, **Premsal Blanc**, and **Giró Ros**.

You'll find local wines featured prominently on restaurant menus across Palma. If you're at a tapas bar or bistro, ask for a **glass of Mallorcan red** to go with your cured meats or grilled lamb. Prefer white? Look for a bottle of **Premsal**, a crisp varietal with notes of green apple and almond.

Some top spots to enjoy Mallorcan wine:

- **Wineing** (Carrer de la Unió, 15): A wine bar with self-serve machines, allowing you to taste over 40 local and international wines by the glass.
- **La Bodeguilla** (Carrer de Sant Jaume, 3): Classic and elegant, with a deep cellar and smart food pairings.
- **Enoteca 1918** (Carrer del Conquistador): A cozy wine shop and bar with staff who love explaining the island's grapes.

If you're interested in wine tourism, many wineries in the central region offer tastings and tours—something worth planning if you have time for a day trip outside the city.

Cocktails and Nightlife: A Stylish Sip

While Palma has its fair share of party spots, its cocktail culture is more sophisticated than you might expect. There are plenty of stylish lounges, hotel rooftops, and moody basement bars where skilled bartenders mix up drinks with precision and flair.

Where to go for a top-tier cocktail:

- **Brass Club** (Passeig Mallorca, 34): Widely regarded as the best cocktail bar in Palma, Brassclub combines sleek design with a menu that includes both classic and experimental drinks. Try the "Coco Chanel," made with rosewater and gin.
- **Chapeau 1987** (Carrer de Sant Jaume): A dimly lit speakeasy with vintage vibes, strong pours, and jazzy ambiance.
- **Sky Bar at Hotel Almudaina**: Perfect for sunset cocktails with panoramic views over the rooftops of the Old Town and the sea.

While gin and tonics remain the island's go-to mixed drink (and the Spanish version often comes in giant balloon glasses), you'll also find cocktails made with local herbs and liqueurs like **Hierbas Mallorquinas**, an aromatic digestif that's sweet, minty, and distinctly Mallorcan.

Want something lighter? Go for a **vermut**, the Spanish version of vermouth that's typically served over ice with a slice of orange or olive.

Café Culture: The Slow Ritual

Coffee in Palma is not just a caffeine fix—it's a daily ritual, a social glue, and sometimes an excuse to take a break and people-watch. Locals don't rush their coffee; they linger over it. Whether it's early morning or mid-afternoon, cafés are always buzzing with conversation and clinking espresso cups.

Types of coffee to know:

- **Café solo** – a strong espresso
- **Cortado** – espresso "cut" with a bit of milk
- **Café con leche** – equal parts espresso and milk, usually for breakfast
- **Carajillo** – espresso with a splash of liquor (typically brandy or rum)

Palma has a mix of old-school cafés with marble tables and vintage tiles, alongside new-wave coffee houses serving single-origin beans and oat milk lattes.

Some favorites across styles:

- **Cafè Riutort** (Carrer del Carme, 32): Cozy, trendy, and known for good coffee and hearty brunches.
- **Rosevelvet Bakery** (Carrer de la Missió, 15): A hit with locals and visitors alike, great coffee and even better cakes.
- **Cafè Cappuccino (Plaça de Cort or Passeig Marítim)**: A local chain with upscale flair—ideal for people-watching in the heart of the city.

The Art of the Terrace

Perhaps the most Mallorcan way to enjoy any drink—wine, coffee, beer, or a cocktail—is on a **terrace**, ideally shaded by an umbrella and surrounded by the murmur of the city. From busy squares to quiet backstreets, nearly every bar and café has some kind of outdoor seating.

And there's a reason locals love it so much: it's where life unfolds. Friends meet, gossip flows, lovers argue, writers scribble in notebooks, and tourists catch their breath between sights. You don't need a plan—just grab a seat and let the pace of the island set in.

Final Thoughts

Drinking in Palma, whether you're sipping espresso at 9 a.m. or finishing your evening with a locally distilled gin, is about more than what's in your glass. It's a social custom, a cultural statement, and a way of experiencing the city in full color. There's elegance, simplicity, and plenty of local flavor woven into every sip.

Chapter 7. Outdoor Activities and Beaches

7.1 Top Beaches Around Palma

Palma de Mallorca's coastline is one of its greatest treasures—stretching out with soft golden sands, turquoise waters, and an atmosphere that ranges from lively and vibrant to peaceful and secluded. Whether you're up for water sports, family time, sunset strolls, or simply relaxing under a parasol with a good book, there's a beach around Palma that fits the bill.

This part of the island may be urbanized, but you're never far from the sea. In fact, one of the joys of Palma is that its best beaches are not only beautiful but also easily accessible.

Here's a closer look at the top beaches in and around Palma that are well worth your time.

1. Playa de Palma

Location: Southeast of Palma city center, stretching for nearly 6 km toward the resort areas of Can Pastilla and El Arenal.

Vibe: Social, active, and ideal for longer beach days

Why go: Playa de Palma is the city's most famous beach—and it lives up to the hype. With wide stretches of soft sand, calm blue water, and a promenade lined with shops, bars, and eateries, this beach has everything you'd expect from a well-equipped urban beach. It's family-friendly, easy to reach by bus or bike, and perfect if you want a mix of sunbathing and social buzz.

What to do there: Rent a lounger and umbrella, join a volleyball game, walk or cycle the beachfront path, or grab an ice cream and people-watch.

2. Cala Major

Location: About 5 km southwest of Palma's city center

Vibe: Cozy, accessible, with a local-meets-tourist feel

Why go: Smaller than Playa de Palma but no less charming, Cala Major offers clear, shallow waters and a pretty setting nestled between low cliffs. It's especially convenient if you're staying nearby or looking for a beach with fewer crowds than the city's main stretch. While surrounded by residential buildings and resorts, it still has a calm, protected feel.

What to do there: Go for a swim in the gentle surf, have lunch at a nearby chiringuito (beach bar), or enjoy a quieter afternoon on soft sand without straying too far from Palma.

3. Can Pere Antoni

Location: Just east of the Palma Cathedral, within walking distance from the Old Town

Vibe: Urban, easygoing, with a great city-sea backdrop

Why go: If you're staying in central Palma and don't feel like hopping on a bus or renting a car, this is your beach. Can Pere Antoni is Palma's "in-town" beach, and while it doesn't match the wild beauty of more remote coves, it offers convenience and postcard views of the cathedral. There's a dedicated bike path nearby, and the beach is popular with joggers, paddleboarders, and locals on lunch breaks.

What to do there: Lounge in the sand with a view of La Seu, take a dip, or grab a coffee from the nearby Es Molinar neighborhood and enjoy the sea breeze.

4. Ciudad Jardín

Location: Along the coastline between Can Pere Antoni and Playa de Palma

Vibe: Laid-back, family-oriented, and mostly local

Why go: This beach has a chilled, residential feel and is a favorite among Palma locals who want a quieter option without heading out of town. It's broad and clean, with a shallow entry into the sea, making it especially good for families with small children. There's a long promenade for walking or rollerblading, and plenty of small cafés nearby.

What to do there: Pack a picnic, watch the sunset, or enjoy a slow morning swim before brunch at one of the beachside eateries.

5. Cala Estancia

Location: Next to Can Pastilla, at the western edge of Playa de Palma

Vibe: Calm, sheltered, and good for swimmers

Why go: This beach sits in a small bay, making the waters extra calm—ideal for relaxed swimming or paddleboarding. It's well-serviced but smaller in size, offering a more intimate beach experience while still being close to Palma's amenities. The sand is soft, and the vibe is low-key.

What to do there: Rent a paddleboard, take in the sunset views, or sip a drink at one of the laid-back cafés overlooking the bay.

6. Illetas Beach (Platja d'Illetes)

Location: About 9 km southwest of Palma, easily reachable by car or bus

Vibe: Upmarket, stylish, and a favorite among locals and in-the-know travelers

Why go: Tucked into a rocky coastline, Illetas Beach offers a bit of Mediterranean glamour. With clear aquamarine water, fine sand, and a couple of chic beach clubs, this is where people go when they want a beach day that's both scenic and serene. The surrounding pine trees provide shade, and the view across the bay is stunning.

What to do there: Book a sunbed at a beach club, snorkel in the crystal-clear waters, or just enjoy a more upscale seaside setting.

7. Portixol Beach

Location: Just a 20-minute walk or a short bike ride east from Palma's cathedral

Vibe: Relaxed, community-oriented, and charming

Why go: This beach isn't as famous as Playa de Palma, but it's beloved by locals for its authenticity. Located near the charming marina neighborhood of Portixol, it feels more like a local hangout than a tourist destination. The beach is smaller and quieter, and the promenade is dotted with trendy cafés and seafood restaurants.

What to do there: Come for a morning swim, then grab brunch at one of the waterfront spots like Ola del Mar or The Nook.

Final Thoughts

The beaches around Palma offer more than just a place to lay your towel—they're part of the city's identity and rhythm. Some are full of life, others are quiet and serene, but all of them let you dip into the Mediterranean lifestyle in your own way. Whether you want sun and sand steps from your hotel or a scenic bay tucked away from the crowds, Palma's coastline delivers the goods.

7.2 Cycling and Walking Routes

Palma de Mallorca is a dream for travelers who like to explore on foot or by bike. The city's layout makes it friendly for both, with scenic seafront promenades, well-marked cycling paths, and charming historic neighborhoods best discovered at a slower pace. Whether you're into active travel, keen on local photography, or just want to work off that extra slice of ensaïmada, there's a trail, walkway, or bike lane waiting for you.

Palma's warm Mediterranean climate—with long dry summers and mild winters—makes it ideal for outdoor exploration nearly all year round. Here's a breakdown of some of the best routes for cyclists and walkers, each offering a different view of Palma's urban charm, coastal beauty, and countryside peace.

Seafront Promenade (Paseo Marítimo)

Type: Easy | Distance: Approx. 10 km | Suitable for: Walking, cycling, jogging

If there's one route that every visitor should do at least once, it's the stretch along the Paseo Marítimo. Starting from the Port of Palma and running east past the Cathedral, beaches, and through to Portixol and El Molinar, this paved seafront path offers some of the best views of the Bay of Palma.

For walkers, it's a relaxing place to take in the sea air and watch yachts drift into the marina. For cyclists, it's an ideal stretch for both casual pedaling and longer rides connecting to nearby coastal towns. The path is wide, well-maintained, and lit in the evenings, making it safe and enjoyable any time of day.

Palma to El Arenal Coastal Route

Type: Moderate | Distance: Approx. 15 km one way | Suitable for: Cycling, e-biking

This scenic coastal ride runs from central Palma all the way to the beach town of El Arenal. It starts on the Paseo Marítimo and follows the coastline past Portixol, Ciudad Jardín, and Playa de Palma.

Along the way, you'll pass beach cafés, wide stretches of sand, palm-lined paths, and local parks. It's a favorite among both locals and visitors for a relaxed day ride—stop along the way for a swim, a cold drink, or just to enjoy the sea breeze. There are multiple bike rental stations and places to rest, so even if you're not an avid cyclist, this one's doable and worth it.

The Old Town Walking Circuit

Type: Easy to moderate | Distance: Flexible (2–5 km) | Suitable for: Walking only

Exploring Palma's Old Town on foot is like stepping into another era. Narrow cobbled lanes weave between centuries-old stone buildings, inner courtyards, hidden chapels, and small plazas where cafés spill onto the pavement. Start near Plaça Major and work your way toward La Seu Cathedral, then wind your way through Carrer dels Apuntadors, past boutique shops, artisan stores, and small bakeries.

Some highlights along the walk include:

- La Rambla, a tree-lined boulevard with flower stalls
- Plaça de Cort, home to Palma's old olive tree and city hall
- The Jewish Quarter, with its atmospheric alleyways and unique history

This walking circuit is less about distance and more about absorbing the details—the architecture, the aromas from bakeries, the way light hits a sandstone wall at golden hour. It's slow travel at its finest.

Bellever Forest Park (Bosque de Bellver)

Type: Moderate | Distance: Approx. 4–6 km | Suitable for: Walking, light hiking, cycling

For a little more nature and a break from the city streets, head to Bellver Forest Park, located around the famous Bellver Castle. This hilly, wooded area is a favorite spot for both joggers and casual walkers. Pine trees shade the trails, and birdsong fills the air. From various lookout points, you'll be treated to panoramic views of Palma Bay, the marina, and the surrounding mountains.

The paths here are well-maintained and vary in incline, making it suitable for families, dog-walkers, and those looking for a peaceful stroll in a natural setting. Cyclists are welcome, too—just be prepared for a few short climbs.

Palma to Sóller (Advanced Ride)

Type: Challenging | Distance: Approx. 30 km (one way) | Suitable for: Experienced cyclists

If you're up for a serious ride, the Palma to Sóller route is a classic. This scenic journey heads inland through the foothills of the Tramuntana Mountains, winding through almond groves, olive orchards, and small towns. The route includes a steady climb and some hairpin turns, so it's best suited for seasoned riders with the stamina for a day on the saddle.

Many riders stop in Bunyola for a break, then continue to the picturesque town of Sóller. For an easier return, you can take the vintage train or bus back to Palma.

Tips for Cyclists and Walkers in Palma

- **Bike Rentals:** Easily found across the city, including electric bike options. Hourly or daily rates are usually affordable.
- **Stay Hydrated:** Especially during warmer months. Always carry water—many public fountains aren't potable.
- **Sun Protection:** Hats, sunglasses, and sunscreen are a must, even for short strolls.
- **Footwear:** Good walking shoes or sandals with grip are ideal for cobbled streets and longer distances.
- **Road Safety:** Cyclists should stick to marked paths where possible and be mindful of traffic in shared zones.
- **Respect Local Pace:** In Old Town, take your time and keep noise to a minimum in residential lanes.

Whether you're biking along the Mediterranean coast or walking the quiet corners of Palma's ancient neighborhoods, exploring the city on foot or two adds depth to your visit. You'll see more, notice the small things, and move at a pace that lets you take it all in.

7.3 Boat Tours and Water Sports

With its turquoise waters, hidden coves, and postcard-perfect coastline, Palma de Mallorca is practically made for water lovers. Whether you're the type to chill on a catamaran, snorkel around underwater rock formations, or try your hand at paddleboarding, there are plenty of options to dive into—literally and figuratively.

Palma's seaside setting along the Bay of Palma means you don't have to travel far to enjoy the water. And the best part? You don't need to be an expert to enjoy most of these activities. Guided tours and equipment rentals are easy to arrange, and the sea is often calm, especially from May to early October.

Let's break it down into the most popular and rewarding aquatic activities you can enjoy in and around Palma.

Scenic Boat Tours and Day Cruises

If you want a relaxed way to enjoy the coastline—with maybe a glass of cava in hand—consider booking a boat tour. These range from short harbor cruises to full-day excursions that include food, swimming stops, and onboard music.

Popular Options:

- **Catamaran Cruises:** Great for groups or couples. Most depart from the marina near the Auditorium or the Paseo Marítimo area and head toward Cala Blava or Illetas, with swim stops and lunch onboard.
- **Sunset Sails:** A romantic favorite. These tours usually last 2–3 hours, timed to coincide with the golden evening light as the sun dips behind the mountains.
- **Glass-Bottom Boats:** Perfect for families with kids or anyone curious about marine life without getting wet. Departures are frequent from Playa de Palma.
- **Private Charters:** Available for a more intimate or customizable experience. Prices vary based on boat size, amenities, and duration, but you can find options ranging from small motorboats to luxury yachts.

Booking Tips:

- Book online in advance during summer months—it gets busy fast.
- Bring a swimsuit, towel, sunblock, and maybe a light jacket for wind.
- Some cruises include lunch or drinks, others don't—check ahead.

Snorkeling and Scuba Diving

Palma's waters might not be as coral-rich as tropical destinations, but you'll still find impressive underwater sights like sea caves, schools of colorful fish, and hidden reefs. A few kilometers out from the city, the water becomes crystal-clear, making it ideal for diving and snorkeling.

Best Snorkeling Areas Near Palma:

- **Cala Blava:** Small coves with rocky seabeds, perfect for spotting fish and sea urchins.
- **Illetas Beach:** Shallow entry, calmer waters, and great visibility.
- **Cala Mayor:** Easy to reach from the city, with rental gear available nearby.

Diving Centers in Palma:

- Multiple PADI-certified dive shops offer beginner and advanced dives, as well as "try dives" for first-timers.
- Common dive sites include shipwrecks, caves, and protected marine parks.
- All equipment is typically provided, and you'll have a guide to ensure safety and fun.

Stand-Up Paddleboarding (SUP) and Kayaking

For a workout with a view, paddleboarding or kayaking gives you a unique angle on the coastline. You can rent gear directly on several beaches or join a guided tour that leads you to sea caves, cliffs, and snorkeling stops.

Where to Go:

- **Portixol & El Molinar:** Calm waters, scenic vibe, and gear rental spots along the promenade.
- **Playa de Palma:** Good for beginners, with long stretches of beach and shallow water.
- **Cala Xinxell (Illetas area):** A bit further out, but excellent for exploring coves.

Tips for First-Timers:

- Early morning is usually calmest, with less wind and boat traffic.
- Wear water shoes or sports sandals.
- Life jackets are typically included and required for rentals.

Jet Skiing and Parasailing

Looking for something a bit more high-octane? Palma's coastline caters to adrenaline lovers too. From May to October, jet ski rentals and parasailing adventures are widely available, especially around Playa de Palma.

Jet Skiing:

- Available with or without a license—if you're license-free, you'll need to join a guided tour.
- Most rides last 20–60 minutes.
- Routes often go past cliffs, caves, or even dolphins if you're lucky.

Parasailing:

- Departures usually take place from the main marina or from beachside kiosks near S'Arenal.
- You'll fly solo or in tandem, and the view from above is unforgettable.
- Most tours last under an hour, but you're airborne for 10–15 minutes.

Sailing Courses and Yacht Rentals

For travelers looking to learn something new or brush up on old skills, several sailing schools around Palma offer multi-day courses or private lessons. If you already have sailing experience, you can rent a yacht or catamaran for a half-day or full-day outing.

Sailing Schools:

- Offer lessons in English, Spanish, and German.
- Choose from beginner courses, family classes, or full certification programs.

Yacht Rentals:

- Can be self-driven with a valid license or skippered for peace of mind.
- Options range from basic sailboats to luxury yachts with crew, meals, and watersports included.

General Tips for Water Activities in Palma

- **Safety First:** Always listen to guides, wear life vests where needed, and respect local regulations.
- **Sun Protection:** The sun reflects off the sea—use waterproof sunscreen and reapply often.
- **Bring Cash:** Smaller rental stands and kiosks may not accept cards.
- **Respect Nature:** Don't touch or take marine life, and be mindful of plastic waste or sunscreen runoff in sensitive ecosystems.

Whether you want to relax, get active, or try something totally new, Palma's waters offer it all. From gentle sailing trips to full-throttle jet skiing, there's a way for every type of traveler to connect with the sea—and you're never more than a few minutes from the shoreline.

7.4 Parks and Green Spaces

Palma de Mallorca might be known for its beaches and historic landmarks, but there's another side to the city that's just as refreshing—its parks and green pockets. Whether you're looking for a quiet place to stroll, a picnic spot, or a shady escape from the midday sun, Palma's gardens and public parks offer a breath of fresh air and a chance to see a more relaxed, everyday side of the city.

You won't find sprawling Central Park–style expenses here, but what Palma lacks in size, it makes up for with charm, Mediterranean greenery, and peaceful corners that often feel worlds away from the urban buzz.

Parc de la Mar

Located just below the iconic La Seu Cathedral, this is probably the best-known green space in the city. It's not so much a "park" in the traditional sense, but rather a large open area by the sea with wide walkways, modern art installations, and a massive artificial lake that reflects the cathedral's towers—making it a favorite photo spot.

Why it's worth a visit:

- Perfect for a leisurely stroll with postcard views.
- Often hosts art festivals, concerts, and outdoor events.
- Nearby cafés make it easy to grab a drink or snack.

You'll often find locals jogging, kids riding scooters, and tourists snapping photos here. In the evenings, it becomes a laid-back social space as the golden light bathes the cathedral and the sea breeze rolls in.

Parc de Sa Riera

This is one of Palma's largest green areas and one of the few that feels like a full-fledged city park. Located just north of the city center, it stretches along a dry riverbed and offers wide, tree-lined paths, grassy areas for lounging, sports courts, and a small skate park.

Ideal for:

- Jogging or walking away from the crowds.
- Families with kids—there are several playgrounds.
- A low-key afternoon with a picnic blanket and a book.

It's not particularly touristy, which makes it a great place to see daily life in Palma. You'll often pass locals walking dogs, reading under trees, or playing paddle tennis.

Jardins de S'Hort del Rei

Tucked beside the Royal Palace of La Almudaina and just below the cathedral, this small formal garden is one of the prettiest corners of the old town. Originally part of the medieval royal orchards, it's now a quiet, shaded escape from the nearby bustle.

Features:

- Ornamental fountains and symmetrical hedges.
- Moorish-style stone arches and tiled benches.
- Ideal for a short break while sightseeing in the historic quarter.

Though it only takes a few minutes to walk through, it's a peaceful detour worth taking—especially on a warm afternoon.

Parc de Ses Estacions

Right across from Palma's main train and bus station, this green zone is often the first slice of nature visitors encounter when arriving from the airport or other parts of the island.

What to expect:

- Central fountain, lots of benches, and tall palms.
- A mix of modern landscaping and traditional gardens.
- Frequent meeting spot for locals, especially young people.

It's not the most scenic of Palma's parks, but it's very practical—good for resting after travel or grabbing some shade before catching a train or bus.

Forest of Bellver (Bosque de Bellver)

This is the city's most expensive natural green space, and it surrounds the iconic Bellver Castle. While most visitors come to see the castle itself, the surrounding pine forest is a destination in its own right.

Highlights:

- Extensive hiking and walking trails, some offering sea views.
- A popular spot for cycling, running, or dog walking.
- Picnic areas and quiet corners among the trees.

If you're up for some light exercise, walking up to the castle through the forest paths is a great way to escape the city streets and enjoy nature without leaving Palma proper.

Other Notable Green Spaces

- **Jardins de la Misericòrdia:** A quiet, shaded courtyard garden near Carrer de la Misericòrdia, perfect for reading or a calm midday break.
- **Jardins de la Torre de l'Amor:** A little-known spot near the city walls with benches and views—more of a hidden gem than a full park.
- **Plaça del Bisbe and Plaça Major:** While technically plazas, these areas have a bit of greenery and plenty of shade from trees and umbrellas—great for sitting with a drink and people-watching.

Tips for Enjoying Palma's Green Spaces

- **Bring water:** Even shady areas can get warm during summer months.
- **Respect siesta hours:** Some smaller parks may be quieter (and almost empty) during early afternoon when locals rest indoors.
- **Mind the pigeons and cats:** Many public parks have a local animal presence—mostly harmless, but be cautious with food.
- **Use sunscreen:** Even in shaded areas, the UV index is strong in Mallorca.

In a city as lively and colorful as Palma, these green escapes offer a welcome balance. Whether you want to stretch your legs, let kids run around, or enjoy a sandwich in peace, you'll find a park or garden to suit your pace. These spaces might not always show up on top-10 lists, but they're part of what makes Palma feel livable, lovely, and, at times, surprisingly serene.

Chapter 8: Day Trips and Excursions

8.1 Valldemossa

Tucked away in the dramatic folds of the Tramuntana Mountains, **Valldemossa** is one of the most enchanting villages on the island of Mallorca—and it's only about 30 minutes from Palma by car or bus. With its honey-colored stone houses, cobbled streets, and forested mountain backdrop, Valldemossa feels like it's been lifted straight from a postcard. It's peaceful, picturesque, and packed with both history and understated charm, making it one of the top day trips from the capital.

Getting There from Palma

The easiest way to reach Valldemossa is by car, and the drive itself is part of the appeal. As you leave Palma, the road winds gently upward through lush countryside and limestone cliffs until you reach the village, perched nearly 1,000 feet above sea level. Parking is relatively straightforward thanks to well-marked public lots on the edge of the village.

If you're traveling by public transport, take the **L210 bus** from the Palma bus station. Buses run several times a day and take roughly 30–40 minutes.

What Makes Valldemossa Special?

This village isn't just about good looks (though there's plenty of that)—it's steeped in cultural and literary history, most famously tied to the composer **Frédéric Chopin** and the writer **George Sand**, who wintered here in the 1830s. Their short but memorable stay put Valldemossa on the cultural map, and today it continues to attract artists, writers, and travelers who crave peace, inspiration, and mountain air.

Top Things to See and Do

Real Cartuja de Valldemossa (Royal Charterhouse)

Once a Carthusian monastery, this striking building complex is the village's main attraction. Originally a royal residence, it was later converted into a monastery in the 14th century. When Chopin and George Sand came to Valldemossa, they rented a room here—an event commemorated with a museum room full of personal artifacts, manuscripts, and even one of Chopin's pianos.

Visitors can explore the chapel, pharmacy, library, gardens, and the adjoining palace rooms. There's also a short piano concert included with admission, often featuring Chopin's music.

- **Admission**: Around €9 (varies by season and events)
- **Opening Hours**: Typically 10:00 AM – 4:00 PM (closed on some holidays)
- **Website**: www.cartujadevalldemossa.com

Wander the Village Streets

The best way to soak up Valldemossa is to simply wander. The steep, narrow lanes are lined with stone façades adorned with bright green shutters and colorful flower pots. Keep an eye out for ceramic plaques with religious imagery on many homes—these are typical of the area and give the village a quaint, reverent feel.

Don't miss **Career Rectoria**, one of the most photogenic streets in the village, or **Plaça de la Cartoixa**, the main square where you'll find cafés and artisan shops.

Chopin and George Sand Cultural Center

A smaller but well-curated museum devoted to their time in Valldemossa, including letters, personal objects, and memorabilia. It gives a fascinating look at their rocky stay and the inspiration the island provided—even if George Sand was not overly fond of the Mallorcan winter.

Cultural Notes and Artisan Crafts

Valldemossa has a strong sense of place. It's not a manufactured tourist village—it's lived in, loved, and preserved.

That's evident in its local crafts scene. You'll find workshops selling handmade ceramics, natural soaps, olive wood products, and local herbal liqueurs. Keep an eye out for **"herbes de Mallorca"**, a sweet or dry anise-based spirit often served after a meal.

Street musicians and painters are a common sight, especially in the warmer months, and the overall pace is slow and unrushed.

Food and Cafés in Valldemossa

You can't leave Valldemossa without trying a **coca de** , a soft, sugar-dusted potato bun that pairs perfectly with hot chocolate or a coffee. These are a specialty of the town and can be found at just about every café.

Recommended Spots:

- **Panaderia Ca'n Molinas**: The most famous bakery in town, known for traditional Mallorcan pastries and a charming garden terrace.
- **Es Roquissar**: A cozy restaurant near the main square offering hearty Mediterranean dishes with local ingredients.
- **Casa de Sa Miranda**: A beautiful little tea room in a quiet side street, known for fresh cakes and herbal teas.

When to Go

Valldemossa can get busy in July and August, so if you're after quiet streets and a cooler breeze, consider visiting in spring or early fall. Early mornings are also ideal if you want to beat the day-tripper rush from Palma and enjoy the silence of the village.

Good to Know

- **Footwear**: Wear comfortable shoes—many streets are cobbled and hilly.
- **Accessibility**: Due to its historic layout, not all areas are wheelchair-friendly, though main squares and most cafés are accessible.
- **Weather**: Slightly cooler than Palma due to its elevation—great in summer, but brings layers in winter.

- **Events**: If you're lucky enough to visit in July, the **Chopin Festival** brings classical music concerts to the monastery, drawing fans from around the world.

Final Thoughts

Valldemossa is the kind of place that slows you down in the best way. It's not about ticking off attractions, but about sitting still long enough to listen to the sound of birds over the rooftops, to smell wild herbs on the breeze, and to let yourself get lost down a quiet alleyway. As far as day trips from Palma go, this one offers that rare mix of beauty, culture, and soul—all in under an hour from the city.

8.2 Sóller and Port de Sóller

A visit to Sóller and its nearby coastal twin, **Port de Sóller**, is like getting two day trips for the price of one. Nestled in a lush valley surrounded by the Tramuntana Mountains and lined with citrus groves, Sóller is one of Mallorca's most beloved inland towns. Just a short tram ride away, the picturesque bay of Port de Sóller offers seaside relaxation, fresh seafood, and a promenade perfect for wandering.

Whether you're after mountain air, historic charm, or Mediterranean sea views, this region delivers. It's easily accessible from Palma and well worth carving out an entire day for.

Getting There from Palma

One of the most popular and scenic ways to reach Sóller is via the **historic wooden train**, known as the **Ferrocarril de Sóller**, which dates back to 1912. The journey itself is part of the experience, winding through olive groves, tunnels, and dramatic mountain landscapes before arriving in Sóller town.

- **Train from Palma to Sóller**: Departs from Palma Estació Intermodal (Plaza de España). The trip takes about **1 hour**.
- **Tram from Sóller to Port de Sóller**: Connects the town and the port in about **15–20 minutes** on an open-air vintage tram.

Alternatively, you can drive or take public buses (TIB line 204), but the train-and-tram combo is iconic for a reason.

Sóller Town Highlights

Plaça de la Constitució

This central square is the beating heart of Sóller, framed by orange trees, cafés, and the imposing **Sant Bartomeu Church**—a striking blend of Gothic and modernist architecture. The tram glides directly through the square, creating a charming old-world atmosphere.

Grab a table at one of the cafés for coffee or lunch, and enjoy some of the best people-watching in Mallorca.

Sant Bartomeu Church

With its intricate stone façade and striking rose window, this church is impossible to miss. Originally built in the 13th century and later redesigned by a disciple of Antoni Gaudí, it's one of the most beautiful religious structures on the island.

Can Prunera Modernist Museum

Located in a beautifully restored modernist mansion, Can Prunera is a small but delightful museum featuring 20th-century art, period furniture, and temporary exhibits. It's also a great place to appreciate Sóller's architectural flair.

- **Admission**: Around €5

- **Opening Hours**: Typically 10:30 AM – 6:00 PM
- **Website**: www.canprunera.com

Saturday Market

If you're visiting on a Saturday, don't miss the town's vibrant **weekly market**, which spills across the main square and surrounding streets. You'll find everything from fresh produce and local cheeses to handmade textiles and ceramics.

Citrus Valley and the Sóller Oranges

Sóller's fertile valley is famed for its **oranges and lemons**, which have been grown here for centuries. These citrus fruits were once exported across Europe, and they still define the landscape today. Many shops sell fresh juice or orange marmalade, and some even offer tastings.

You can also visit **Ecovinyassa**, a citrus farm that offers guided tours of the orchards, tastings, and a peaceful garden to relax in. Reservations are usually required.

Port de Sóller: The Coastal Side

Just down the hill from the town, Port de Sóller offers a complete change of scenery—coastal views, fresh sea air, and a relaxed, sun-drenched vibe.

The Bay and Beaches

The port curves gently around a horseshoe-shaped bay flanked by two small beaches: **Platja d'en Repic** and **Platja des Través**. Both are family-friendly, sandy, and relatively calm thanks to the sheltered location.

It's ideal for swimming, sunbathing, or just strolling along the promenade with an ice cream in hand.

Passeig Es Través Promenade

Lined with cafés, restaurants, and small shops, this pedestrian-friendly walkway is perfect for an afternoon wander. You'll find everything from casual eateries to upscale seafood restaurants offering local specialties like **caldereta de langosta** (lobster stew) and grilled catch-of-the-day.

Maritime Museum and Lighthouses

For those curious about the area's nautical past, the **Museu de la Mar** in an old chapel tells the story of Sóller's seafaring history. If you're up for a bit of walking, head toward the **Far de Cap Gros**, a scenic lighthouse on the western headland with panoramic views of the bay.

Tips for Visiting

- **Best Time to Go**: Spring (March–May) is ideal—wildflowers are blooming, the citrus groves are fragrant, and the area isn't yet overrun by high-season crowds.
- **Footwear**: Comfortable walking shoes are essential if you plan to explore both the town and the port.
- **Dining**: If you're staying for dinner, Port de Sóller is especially charming in the early evening, when the sun sets over the bay.
- **Souvenirs**: Don't leave without trying or buying **orange blossom honey**, **artisan soaps**, or local olive oil.

Final Thoughts

Sóller and Port de Sóller together offer a perfect blend of inland tradition and seaside serenity. The mix of dramatic scenery, charming architecture, slow-paced lifestyle, and easy connections from Palma make this one of Mallorca's most rewarding day trips. Whether you're coming for a nostalgic train ride, a scenic lunch by the water, or a stroll through orange-scented lanes, this area leaves a lasting impression.

8.3 Serra de Tramuntana

The **Serra de Tramuntana**, a rugged mountain range stretching along the northwestern coast of Mallorca, is more than just a pretty backdrop — it's the island's wild heart. Recognized as a UNESCO World Heritage Site for its cultural landscape, the range is a tapestry of terraced hillsides, dry-stone walls, ancient olive groves, scenic villages, and winding cliffside roads that defy logic and physics.

Whether you're a hiker, a road-tripper, a nature-lover, or someone who just wants to take in postcard-perfect views without breaking a sweat, the Tramuntana has something for you.

Where It Is and How to Get There

The Tramuntana range runs from **Andratx** in the southwest to **Cap de Formentor** in the northeast, forming a dramatic spine that separates the coast from the central plains. You can reach its more popular sections by car or guided tour, though public transport also connects major towns like **Sóller**, **Valldemossa**, and **Pollença**.

- From Palma, it takes about:
    - 25 minutes to **Valldemossa**
    - 45 minutes to **Deià**

○ 1 hour to **Pollença**

Driving through the MA-10 highway is a highlight in itself, offering hairpin turns, deep gorges, sea cliffs, and dramatic overlooks — a dream (or a challenge) for road trip lovers.

Why It's Worth the Trip

There are mountain ranges, and then there's the **Serra de Tramuntana**. This isn't just about elevation — it's about atmosphere. The scenery flips between alpine and Mediterranean. You'll see stone villages clinging to cliffs, goats perched impossibly high above the trail, and hikers stopping mid-trek not for a break but to stare in disbelief at the views.

Add in historic monasteries, hidden coves, citrus orchards, and lookouts where you feel like you're standing at the edge of the world — and you've got the makings of one unforgettable adventure.

Highlights and Must-Visit Spots

Valldemossa

Famous for its monastery and cobbled streets lined with flower pots, this village is where **Frédéric Chopin** and **George Sand** spent a stormy winter in 1838. Even now, it feels preserved in time. Walk its narrow lanes, visit the Royal Charterhouse, and try a coca de patata (a local sweet bun) with thick hot chocolate.

Deià

This bohemian cliffside village has long attracted artists, musicians, and writers. With stunning views, stone houses, and a laid-back air, Deià is also home to Cala Deià, a small rocky beach and seafood haven that's pure Mediterranean bliss.

Sóller and Port de Sóller

Nestled in an orange-filled valley, Sóller is connected by vintage train to Palma and by tram to its coastal port. It's the perfect base for hikes and short road trips deeper into the range.

Fornalutx

Often called one of the prettiest villages in Spain, Fornalutx is a tiny hamlet of stone houses and narrow steps, draped in bougainvillea and surrounded by the Tramuntana's peaks. It's a quiet spot, perfect for those wanting a less touristy but deeply authentic feel.

Sa Calobra and Torrent de Pareis

A serpentine drive or boat trip leads to Sa Calobra, a dramatic beach set between steep cliffs. From there, hike into the **Torrent de Pareis**, a natural gorge that opens to the sea. It's a truly cinematic landscape, though it can be challenging — sturdy shoes and good weather are essential.

Lluc Monastery

Tucked into the higher elevations, the **Monestir de Lluc** has been a pilgrimage site for centuries. It's peaceful, spiritual, and surrounded by excellent hiking trails. You can even stay overnight in one of the monastery's guest rooms.

Hiking and Outdoor Adventures

The **GR-221 Dry Stone Route** (Ruta de Pedra en Sec) is a long-distance hiking path that winds through the Tramuntana, covering over 170 kilometers. You don't need to do it all — many visitors choose short sections, like:

- **Deià to Sóller** (approx. 3–4 hours): Coastal views, stone paths, and ancient olive trees.
- **Sóller to Biniaraix and Barranc de Biniaraix**: A circular route with a dramatic gorge and terraced scenery.
- **Cúber Reservoir to Lluc**: Peaceful, high-altitude terrain with views that stretch across the island.

Most trails are marked, but it's wise to carry a local hiking map, plenty of water, and sun protection. Early spring and autumn are ideal for hiking due to cooler weather and fewer crowds.

Cycling the Tramuntana

Mallorca is a mecca for cyclists, and Tramuntana is the crown jewel. Professional teams train here in winter, but there are routes for all levels:

- **Coll de Sóller**: A popular but steep pass with hairpin turns and epic views.
- **Sa Calobra Climb**: One of Europe's most famous ascents — 26 hairpins over 10km.
- **Andratx to Pollença (via MA-10)**: A full-day challenge, but a stunner.

You can rent road bikes in Palma or Sóller, and many hotels in the area cater specifically to cyclists.

Food, Culture, and Local Life

While the Tramuntana dazzles with natural beauty, it also carries deep-rooted Mallorcan traditions. You'll find small **family-run restaurants** serving local dishes like (a vegetable bake), **pa amb oli** (bread with oil, tomatoes, and ham), and **suckling pig**. In villages, it's common to see farmers tending olive groves, or hear locals chatting in Mallorquín.

Markets pop up on different days — Sóller's is on Saturdays, while Valldemossa's is on Sundays — offering local cheeses, honey, herbs, and handwoven baskets.

Tips for Visiting

- **Driving Skills Needed**: If you rent a car, be prepared for narrow roads and sharp curves. Take it slow, and be respectful of cyclists.
- **Avoid High Season Congestion**: Try to arrive early in summer or consider a spring/autumn visit when it's cooler and less crowded.
- **Stay Overnight**: Consider booking a rural hotel (finca), monastery, or boutique inn to enjoy the peaceful atmosphere after the day-trippers leave.
- **Pack for Layers**: Weather in the mountains can change quickly — bring light layers and a waterproof jacket.

Final Thoughts

The Serra de Tramuntana isn't just a mountain range — it's a journey through Mallorca's soul. Whether you're gazing over the sea from a mountain road, walking through an olive grove older than some countries, or sipping coffee in a quiet village square, the sense of place here is profound.

It's raw and refined, spiritual and wild — and if you give it the time, it will give you memories you won't forget.

Chapter 9. Shopping and Local Products

9.1 Markets and Artisan Goods

Palma de Mallorca is more than just beaches, architecture, and nightlife — it's also a fantastic place to shop, especially if you're interested in handmade goods, local specialties, and traditional craftsmanship. The markets and artisan boutiques throughout the city give you a chance to see the creative and culinary side of Mallorca up close. From centuries-old crafts to modern interpretations of island life, Palma's shopping scene has something for everyone — and it's refreshingly rooted in authenticity.

Palma's Traditional Markets

Markets in Palma are not just about shopping — they're community spaces where locals buy groceries, vendors share stories, and visitors get a taste of daily Mallorcan life. They're also where tradition and modernity meet, especially as some historic markets have been revamped into hip food halls and cultural venues.

Mercat de l'Olivar

- **Location**: Plaça de l'Olivar, just off Plaça d'Espanya.
- **Established**: 1951
- **Open**: Monday–Saturday, 7 a.m. to 3 p.m. (some stalls reopen for evening tapas around 6 p.m.)

This is Palma's flagship indoor food market — a vibrant, noisy, colorful place where locals shop for the freshest fish, meat, produce, cheese, spices, olives, and baked goods. You'll also find tapas bars and oyster stands where you can sit down for a quick bite and a glass of cava. Don't miss the local sobrasada (paprika-spiced sausage), Mahón cheese, and salt from the nearby salt flats.

Mercat de Santa Catalina

- **Location**: Santa Catalina neighborhood
- **Open**: Monday–Saturday, 7 a.m. to 5 p.m.

Smaller and trendier than Mercat de l'Olivar, Santa Catalina's market reflects its neighborhood vibe: bohemian, creative, and a little upscale. Alongside fresh produce and seafood, there are sushi stalls, boutique wine shops, and gourmet tapas counters. You'll often find expats mingling with chefs doing their morning shopping.

Pere Garau Market

- **Location**: Carrer de Pere Garau, east of Old Town
- **Open**: Monday–Saturday, 6 a.m. to 2 p.m.

Less touristy and more utilitarian, this market is where you'll find real-deal local life. The mix of traditional Mallorcan produce and multicultural vendors gives it an urban, working-class flavor. Expect to see spices, dried legumes, handmade baskets, plants, and a dizzying variety of olives.

Artisan Goods: What to Look For

Mallorca has a rich legacy of traditional crafts, and Palma is one of the best places to shop for items that make great souvenirs or gifts — things that actually feel meaningful and personal, rather than mass-produced.

Textiles and Embroidery

One of the most recognizable products is the *roba de llengües*, or "tongue cloth." This is a centuries-old Mallorcan fabric dyed using a traditional ikat technique. You'll see it in tablecloths, pillow covers, handbags, and espadrilles.

Look for:

- **Teixits Vicens** (available at some Palma boutiques or their store in Pollença)
- **Bujosa Textil** (family-run workshop in Santa Maria del Camí, but sold in Palma shops too)

Ceramics and Pottery

Mallorcan ceramics often feature natural colors and Mediterranean motifs — think olive branches, sea life, and sunburst patterns. Some shops still carry handmade clay cookware, like traditional *greixoneres* (earthenware pots).

Best places to browse:

- Artisan stores in Palma's Old Town or Santa Catalina
- Specialty boutiques like **Cerámica Riera**

Leather Goods

While **Inca** (just inland from Palma) is the historical leather capital of the island, you'll find plenty of artisan leatherwork in Palma itself — including belts, sandals, bags, and wallets.

Notable brands and shops:

- **Camper Lab** – An upscale spin on the iconic Mallorcan shoe brand
- **Mianella** – Handmade leather sandals and handbags

Jewelry

Local designers often draw inspiration from the island's nature and history. Look out for sea glass, pearls, olive wood, and filigree silverwork.

- **Majorica Pearls** – Though technically imitation, they're world-renowned and made in Mallorca since the late 1800s.
- **Local designer boutiques** – Scattered throughout Old Town and Paseo del Borne

Olive Wood Products

Olive wood is valued for its rich grain and durability, and you'll find it used in everything from salad bowls and cheese boards to utensils and ornaments. These make excellent kitchen gifts and are easy to pack.

Shops to check:

- Craft stalls in Plaça Major
- Artisan stores near the Cathedral or along Carrer de Sant Miquel

Seasonal Craft Fairs and Pop-Ups

Throughout the year, Palma hosts craft markets and seasonal fairs that bring together independent artisans and makers from around the island. These are great opportunities to pick up one-of-a-kind items and talk directly to the creators.

- **Fira del Ram** (Spring): Includes craft stalls, though more of a festival atmosphere.
- **Christmas Markets** (Late November to early January): Plaça Major, Plaça d'Espanya, and La Rambla light up with stalls selling handmade ornaments, nativity scenes, ceramics, and winter treats.
- **Plaça Major Craft Market**: Small artisan booths set up regularly (typically mornings) in the square, selling leather, lace, jewelry, and painted tiles.

Tips for Market and Artisan Shopping

- **Bargaining**: Unlike in many markets around the world, haggling isn't common or expected in Palma — especially with artisan goods.
- **Cash Is Handy**: While many stalls accept cards, it's smart to carry some euros, especially in smaller markets or for low-cost items.
- **Ask Questions**: Most artisans are happy to talk about their work and explain their process. Don't be shy — it often adds meaning to what you buy.
- **Look for "Products Balear"**: This label marks items made in the Balearic Islands, assuring quality and authenticity.

9.2 Best Streets for Boutique Shopping

If you're after something more curated than a market and more personal than a department store, Palma de Mallorca's boutique shopping scene will keep you entertained for hours — or days, honestly. Tucked between the city's historic buildings and modern cafes are dozens of independent shops selling everything from handmade jewelry to island-inspired fashion, artisanal decor, and high-end design. And the best part? You don't have to wander aimlessly — Palma has several neighborhoods and streets that are known as hotspots for boutique shopping.

Whether you're searching for locally crafted pieces or the latest European trends, these streets are where you'll find Palma's style and creativity on full display.

Passeig del Born (Paseo del Borne)

Often called the "Golden Mile" of Palma, Passeig del Born is more than just a shopping street — it's one of the city's most beautiful avenues, lined with grand plane trees, historic stone benches, and elegant buildings. While this boulevard is home to international fashion houses like Louis Vuitton, Carolina Herrera, and Hugo Boss, you'll also find chic Mallorcan boutiques that blend local flair with contemporary style.

Look for:

- **Massimo Dutti and Mango** — Flagship stores often stock more premium selections than other branches.
- **Rialto Living** — A standout lifestyle boutique in a restored 18th-century mansion, offering fashion, homeware, books, art, and a cozy in-house café.

Why shop here: The atmosphere is elegant, open, and energetic. Even window shopping feels luxurious. A great place to start your shopping walk.

Avinguda Jaume III

Just around the corner from Passeig del Born, this wide and stately avenue is a go-to spot for more classic and upscale shopping. Think Spanish department stores, branded shops, and polished accessories.

What to expect:

- Fashion and accessories stores like Bimba y Lola, Uterqüe, and Cortefiel
- Jewelers and eyewear stores
- Bookshops and perfumeries

Tip: The nearby El Corte Inglés department store (on Avinguda d'Alexandre Rosselló, a short walk away) can also be worth visiting for luxury goods, local wines, cosmetics, and gourmet souvenirs — all under one roof.

Carrer de Sant Miquel

This busy pedestrian shopping street connects Plaça d'Espanya with the Old Town and is lined with a mix of chain stores, local brands, and casual boutiques. It's one of the best streets to visit if you're after something practical but stylish — and there's always good people-watching.

You'll find:

- Spanish fashion staples like Stradivarius, Bershka, and Pull & Bear
- Local shoe shops and accessories boutiques
- Small artisan stalls near Plaça Major

Don't miss: Pop into **La Pajarita**, one of Palma's oldest confectioneries, for a taste of Mallorcan marzipan or candied fruits while you shop.

Carrer de la Missió & Surrounding Alleys

For a more off-the-beaten-path experience, wander into the Old Town's narrow streets — particularly around Carrer de la Missió, Carrer de Can Veri, and Carrer de Sant Gaietà. This area offers a more intimate boutique feel, away from crowds, and often feels like a treasure hunt.

Here you'll come across:

- Concept stores blending fashion, art, and design
- Jewelry makers selling handmade, Mediterranean-inspired pieces
- Independent art galleries and gift shops

One highlight: **Estilo Sant Feliu** — a boutique that mixes interior decor with fashion and handmade accessories. It's a great place to find something truly unique.

Santa Catalina Neighborhood

While Santa Catalina is better known for its food scene and lively nightlife, it also has a growing collection of indie shops and urban-style boutiques, many owned by young designers or creative expats.

Expect:

- Boho-chic fashion
- Island-themed decor and handmade candles
- Trendy sunglasses and eco-conscious accessories

This is the place to go if you're looking for a laid-back shopping stroll mixed with coffee stops and lunch at a tapas bar.

Carrer del Sindicat

Running parallel to Carrer de Sant Miquel, this street is slightly less busy but still buzzing with a mix of fashion, shoe stores, and small boutiques. It's a solid option if you want to avoid the more commercial chains and look for more affordable finds.

Fun stop: Several leather goods stores and watch shops line this street — and occasionally you'll find sidewalk sales or outlet-style deals.

La Rambla

Not to be confused with the one in Barcelona, Palma's La Rambla is a pretty, tree-lined promenade running from the Old Town to the Avinguda de Portugal. It's especially good for florists and seasonal pop-ups, but also has art shops and bookstands that give it a creative feel.

If you're in town during spring or Christmas, it's often home to temporary markets and artisan stalls.

Shopping Tips for Boutique Lovers

- **Opening Hours**: Many independent boutiques close during the afternoon (usually between 2 p.m. and 4:30 p.m.) and reopen in the evening. Plan your shopping trips accordingly.

- **Language**: Most shopkeepers speak some English, but trying a few words in Spanish or Catalan is always appreciated.
- **Packaging**: Boutiques in Palma tend to go the extra mile with elegant packaging — ideal if you're buying gifts.
- **Tax-Free Shopping**: Non-EU travelers can claim VAT refunds on purchases over a certain amount. Ask for the "tax-free" form at checkout.

Palma is not just a city of culture and sunshine — it's also a city of style, with a distinct sense of design and artistry that comes through in its shopping streets. Whether you're a casual browser or a fashion-savvy traveler, strolling these streets offers a delightful way to connect with the island's personality.

9.3 Local Souvenirs and What to Buy

No trip to Palma de Mallorca is truly complete without taking a piece of the island home with you. Whether you're shopping for meaningful gifts, unique keepsakes, or just something to remember the salty breeze and golden sun, Mallorca offers a treasure trove of souvenirs beyond the usual postcards and fridge magnets.

The island's strong artisanal tradition, Mediterranean identity, and centuries-old craftsmanship shine through in everything from ceramics and leather goods to traditional food items and handmade textiles.

Here's a well-rounded look at the most authentic and memorable things to buy while you're in Palma — the kind of souvenirs that don't just sit on a shelf but tell a story.

1. Mallorcan Ceramics (Cerámica Mallorquina)

Handcrafted pottery has long been part of the island's heritage. You'll see plates, bowls, and jugs adorned with rustic, earthy glazes and Mediterranean designs — often in bold blues, greens, and yellows.

What to look for:

- **Greixoneres** – traditional terracotta casserole dishes
- Colorful tiled trivets or coasters
- Hand-painted plates with floral or geometric patterns

Where to buy:
Boutiques in Palma Old Town, artisan markets, and shops like "Cerámicas Terracuita" or "La Pajarita."

Tip: These ceramics are often hand-painted and one-of-a-kind. Ask if they're food-safe or decorative only, depending on your plans.

2. Ensaimadas

This spiral-shaped pastry is Mallorca's most iconic baked goods. It's buttery, flaky, and lightly dusted with powdered sugar — and it makes a delicious souvenir for friends or family (or yourself on the plane).

What to know:

- Traditional filling: plain (lisa)
- Others include pumpkin jam (cabello de ángel), chocolate, or custard
- Can be packed in special boxes designed for air travel

Where to buy:
Look for reputable bakeries like **Forn des Teatre**, **Horno Santo Cristo**, or **Can Joan de S'Aigo** — one of Palma's oldest and most beloved cafés.

3. Mallorcan Olive Oil and Sea Salt

Thanks to its fertile soil and Mediterranean climate, Mallorca produces some seriously good olive oil. Paired with locally harvested sea salt, it's a gourmet souvenir that'll instantly bring you back to the island with just one taste.

Try:

- **Flor de Sal d'Es Trenc** – artisanal sea salt often blended with herbs, citrus, or hibiscus
- Extra virgin olive oil from the **Serra de Tramuntana** region, often sold in ceramic bottles

Where to buy:
Specialty shops in Palma like "Oli de Mallorca" or gourmet sections at El Corte Inglés.

4. Handmade Leather Goods

Leather-making has been a Mallorcan tradition for centuries, particularly in towns like Inca and Alaró, just inland from Palma. From belts and bags to sandals and wallets, the quality is excellent — and the designs often lean toward timeless rather than trendy.

Top items:

- Menorquinas (traditional leather sandals)
- Hand-stitched bags, clutches, and belts
- Leather-bound notebooks or accessories

Where to find:
Shops like **Camper Lab**, **Tony Mora**, or **Munper** near Palma center. Or visit the Inca Leather Market on Thursdays if you're open to a short trip.

5. Glassware from Gordiola or Lafiore

Mallorca has a long tradition of blown glass, with roots dating back to the 18th century. The pieces are colorful, imperfect in the best way, and full of character.

Best buys:

- Vases, wine glasses, and decorative bottles
- Swirled glass ornaments and candleholders

Where to get them:
Visit the **Gordiola Glass Factory** in Algaida (just outside Palma) or shop in Palma boutiques carrying **Lafiore** designs.

6. Textiles: Ikat Fabrics (Teles de Llengües)

These bright, flame-like patterned fabrics are made using a centuries-old dyeing technique and are unique to Mallorca. They're often used in upholstery, cushions, and table runners.

Ideas for souvenirs:

- Cushion covers
- Tote bags or fabric pouches
- Table runners or placemats

Where to shop:
 Visit **Teixits Vicens** (based in Pollença, with some stock in Palma stores), or boutiques in the Old Town.

7. Local Wines and Liqueurs

Mallorca's wine scene has grown impressively in the past decade, especially in the Binissalem and Pla i Llevant regions. You'll find crisp whites, bold reds, and some beautifully aromatic rosés — often unavailable outside the island.

Also worth considering is **Hierbas Mallorquinas**, a local herbal liqueur traditionally made with fennel, orange peel, rosemary, and other island herbs. It's served as a digestif and varies from sweet to dry.

Where to buy:
 Wine shops like **La Vinoteca**, **Bodega Santa Clara**, or most gourmet stores around the Old Town.

8. Perfume and Beauty Products Made Locally

Several boutique perfumers and apothecaries now produce products infused with native plants like rosemary, orange blossom, and fig. They're often organic and sold in elegant packaging.

Look for:

- Natural soaps, oils, and solid perfumes
- Skincare lines using Mallorcan olive oil or sea minerals

Shops to check out: **Flor de Sal's beauty line**, **Campos de Ibiza** products, or small perfumeries around Carrer de Sant Feliu.

9. Local Art and Photography

If you prefer your souvenirs wall-mounted, Palma's galleries and art markets offer pieces created by local painters, printmakers, and photographers. Many artists take inspiration from the island's landscapes, sea views, and architecture.

Where to browse:
 Galleries like **Galería Kewenig**, **Gallery RED**, or **Es Baluard's shop** sell pieces from emerging and established artists.

Tips for Buying Souvenirs in Palma

- **Ask about authenticity**: Many shops display "Made in Mallorca" or "Artesanía de Mallorca" labels. It's worth verifying if you want true local craftsmanship.
- **Pack smart**: Wine, olive oil, and ceramics are great gifts, but be sure to pack them securely or ask for travel-safe packaging.
- **Support local**: Markets and artisan shops are often family-run or artist-owned. Shopping here not only means better souvenirs — it means your euros stay on the island.

From edible delights to artisanal keepsakes, Palma offers souvenirs with real heart and heritage. Whether you're loading your suitcase with hand-painted ceramics or just tucking a bottle of salt into your carry-on, each piece brings you closer to the island's spirit long after you've returned home.

9.4 Mallorcan Fashion and Craft

Mallorca isn't just a beach destination or a postcard-perfect island — it's also a place where traditional craftsmanship intersects with a thriving modern fashion scene. In Palma, you'll find everything from high-end designer boutiques and concept stores to humble ateliers where artisans still handcraft textiles, jewelry, shoes, and homewares. There's a genuine pride in heritage here, with many local brands drawing on Mallorcan traditions to create contemporary pieces that feel both rooted and refined.

If you're curious about what makes fashion and craft unique in Mallorca, this guide offers a look at the island's most iconic styles, makers, and what to watch for when shopping.

Mallorcan Footwear: Tradition Meets Style

One of the island's most iconic contributions to fashion is its traditional footwear — especially the **"avarcas"** and **"menorquinas"**, simple, durable sandals originally designed for farmers and laborers. While their origins lie in Menorca, Mallorca has made them its own, with local labels offering modern variations.

Top brands to look for:

- **Castell Menorca** – Offers timeless styles in leather and suede
- **Mibo** – Known for colorful, updated designs
- **Camper** – Probably the most famous Mallorcan footwear brand globally, blending avant-garde design with practicality. Camper's headquarters are based in Inca, and their flagship store in Palma often carries exclusive designs.

For something dressier, **Tony Mora** in Alaró crafts handmade cowboy boots and fine leather shoes using time-honored techniques.

Ikat Weaving: Teles de Llengües

The **"Telas de Lenguas"** (Flame Stitch Ikat) is a textile tradition unique to Mallorca. These fabrics, instantly recognizable by their blurred, flame-like patterns, have been handwoven for centuries using a dye-resist technique that gives them their signature appearance. They're durable and visually striking — used in home decor, accessories, and occasionally clothing.

Top names:

- **Teixits Vicens** (Pollença): Still using wooden looms and natural dyes. You'll find cushions, tote bags, aprons, and fabric by the meter.
- **Bujosa Artesania Textil** (Santa Maria del Camí): Another family-owned workshop producing these fabrics with exquisite craftsmanship.

If you're into slow fashion or love textile arts, a visit to one of their studios or Palma's design boutiques is worth your time.

Jewelry: Locally Designed, Island-Inspired

Mallorca has long been known for **pearl production**, but the island's jewelry scene goes well beyond faux pearls. Local artisans create bold, minimalist, and boho-chic pieces using silver, gold, natural stones, and organic shapes that reflect the sea and land.

Highlights include:

- **Majorica Pearls**: Though technically not natural, these man-made pearls have become a Mallorcan icon, and the factory store in Manacor is popular for gifts and timeless styles.
- **Gema Correa**: A Palma-based designer who crafts elegant and symbolic pieces with a modern edge.
- **Joyería Forteza**: A local jeweler with decades of tradition, offering high-quality rings, pendants, and earrings with both classic and Mediterranean-inspired flair.

Contemporary Fashion and Independent Designers

Mallorca has been attracting creatives and designers for decades, and Palma, in particular, is now home to a vibrant fashion scene that combines Mediterranean minimalism with ethical and sustainable values.

Concept Stores & Designers to Watch:

- **Pink Flamingos Vintage Market**: A quirky and curated collection of vintage clothing and accessories.
- **Suite 13**: A Palma-based brand offering sustainable fashion with soft, breathable fabrics in relaxed silhouettes — all made in limited batches.
- **Rialto Living**: More than just a lifestyle store — here you'll find fashion, art, books, and design items sourced from across the island and beyond. It's housed in a beautifully restored 18th-century building.
- **Corte Inglés Designer Floor**: While more mainstream, this department store also carries collections by emerging Spanish designers and popular local labels.

Leather Craftsmanship

Mallorca's leatherwork, particularly from the town of **Inca**, is renowned for its attention to detail and quality. While the town itself is home to major outlets, many Palma boutiques carry select items — bags, belts, wallets, or travel accessories — all handmade and often dyed with natural colors.

Look for:

- Hand-sewn details
- Minimalist, functional styles
- Vegetable-tanned leather with a rich patina

If you have time to venture inland, the **Inca Leather Market** (held weekly) is a great spot to pick up handmade leather goods at fair prices.

Home Decor and Artisan Products

Fashion extends into the home, and Mallorca has a strong tradition of handcrafted decor and furnishings that blend rustic aesthetics with island warmth. Woven baskets, palm leaf rugs, handmade pottery, handblown glass, and olive-wood carvings are all part of the local craft scene.

Where to find them:

- **Livingdreams (Santa Maria del Camí):** A beautiful showroom of artisan furniture and homewares
- **Es Baluard Shop:** Sells curated design objects and art-inspired crafts
- **Fet a Sóller:** Features handmade soaps, oils, and natural home products with locally sourced ingredients

Fashion and Craft Events in Palma

If you're in town during key times of year, watch for pop-up markets and artisan fairs such as:

- **Fira de la Llonganissa (Easter Season)** – with craft and food stalls
- **Fira de Nadal (Christmas Markets)** – offers an abundance of handcrafted ornaments and local gifts
- **Nit de l'Art (September)** – though focused on contemporary art, many fashion designers and craftspeople open their studios

Tips for Ethical and Meaningful Shopping

- **Look for the "Artesanía de Mallorca" label** — This official stamp certifies products made using traditional techniques by local artisans.
- **Buy small batches** — Many items sold in boutiques or studios are limited-run or made to order. Don't expect mass production — that's part of the charm.
- **Ask the maker** — Many shopkeepers are also the designers or artists. Ask about their materials and methods — you'll walk away with a richer connection to your purchase.

Whether you're seeking clothing that reflects the relaxed rhythm of the island, accessories rooted in heritage, or one-of-a-kind artisanal pieces, Palma de Mallorca offers a fashion and craft scene that's both soulful and stylish. It's not just about looking good — it's about carrying home a piece of the island's creative spirit.

Chapter 10. Practical Information & Appendix

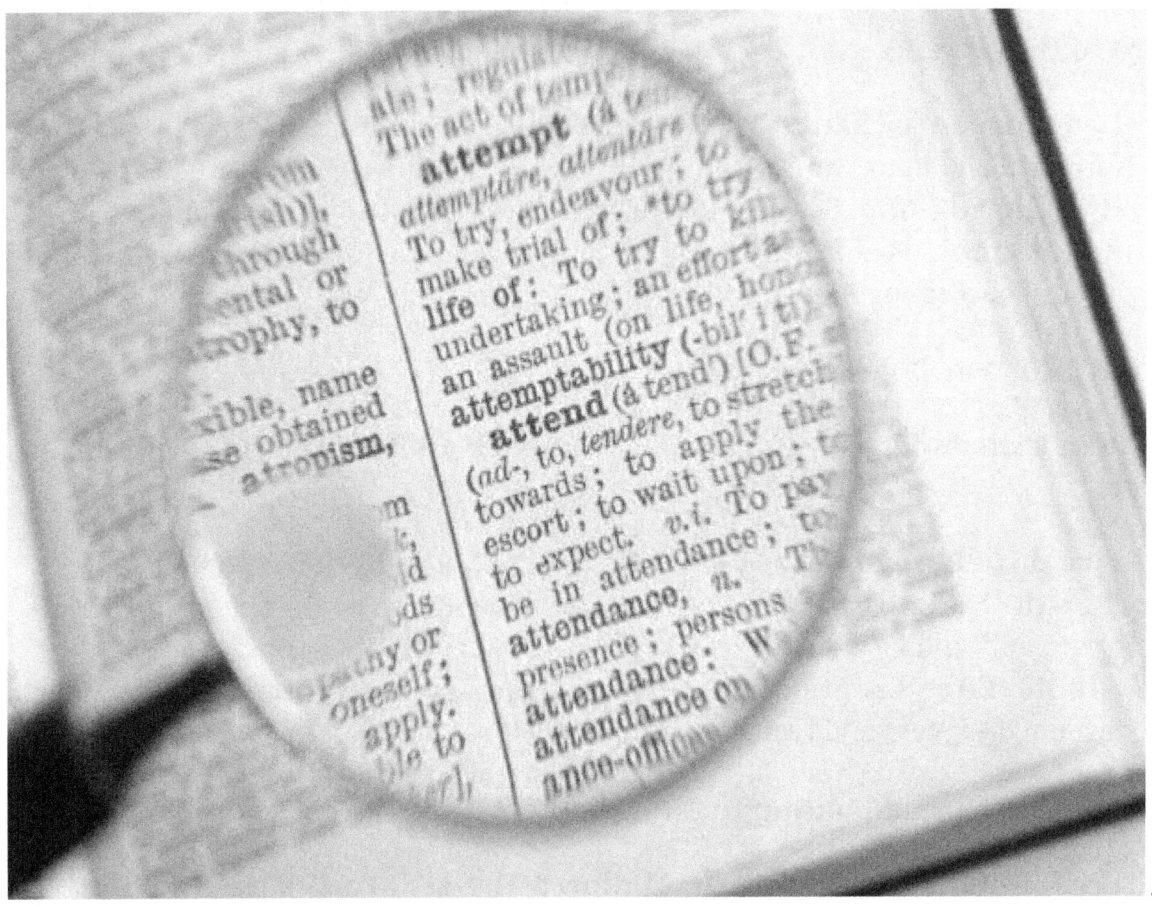

10.1 Currency, Costs, and Budgeting

Understanding how money works in Palma de Mallorca—and planning accordingly—can make the difference between a smooth trip and a series of small frustrations. This section breaks down everything you need to know about the local currency, typical daily expenses, banking options, and practical budgeting tips to help you travel confidently.

Currency in Palma de Mallorca

Mallorca uses the **euro (€)**, which is the official currency of Spain and much of the European Union. Euro banknotes come in denominations of €5, €10, €20, €50, €100, €200, and €500, though the larger bills are rarely used in everyday transactions. Coins range from 1 cent to €2.

Currency code: EUR
Symbol: €

If you're arriving from outside the eurozone, it's important to check the exchange rate ahead of your trip.

Rates can fluctuate, and while airport exchanges are convenient, they typically offer poor value. You're better off using ATMs or your bank card once in Palma—more on that below.

Cash or Card?

Palma is a modern city, and **credit and debit cards are widely accepted**, even for small transactions at cafes, taxis, and retail stores. That said, carrying a small amount of cash is useful for:

- Local markets
- Public restrooms (some charge €0.50–€1)
- Small beach bars or kiosks
- Tipping in restaurants or for tour guides

Look for signs that say "**Tarjeta mínima**" (minimum card payment), which typically means you need to spend at least €5–10 to use a card.

Contactless payments are common across the island, so Apple Pay, Google Pay, and other mobile wallets work in most places.

ATM Access and Banking

ATMs are easy to find throughout Palma—especially in central districts like Old Town, Santa Catalina, and near the port. Most machines offer language options, and many are available 24/7.

- **Withdrawal fees**: Spanish ATMs often charge a fee for foreign cards. This fee is displayed before the transaction is processed—usually between €2 and €5.
- **Bank ATMs vs. Independent ATMs**: Stick to machines operated by major banks like Santander, CaixaBank, BBVA, or Bankia. Avoid independent machines (such as Euronet), which tend to charge higher fees and use unfavorable exchange rates.

Tip: Always choose to be charged in euros instead of your home currency when given the option at ATMs or card terminals. This avoids Dynamic Currency Conversion, which usually results in worse rates.

Typical Daily Costs in Palma

The cost of travel in Palma can vary depending on your travel style, season, and preferences. Here's a general guide to what you can expect for a full day:

Budget Traveler (€60–€90/day)

- Dorm bed or basic hostel: €20–€35
- Simple meals and street food: €15–€25
- Public transport or walking: €5–€10
- Attractions (some free or discounted): €10–€15
- Total: ~€60–€90/day

Mid-Range Traveler (€120–€180/day)

- Boutique hotel or mid-range Airbnb: €70–€110
- Sit-down meals and tapas: €25–€40
- Occasional taxi or scooter rental: €10–€20
- Museum or guided tour: €15–€25
- Total: ~€120–€180/day

Luxury Traveler (€250+/day)

- High-end hotel or resort: €200–€500+
- Fine dining: €60–€100+
- Private transport, boat rental, spa visits: €50–€200
- High-end shopping or experiences: varies widely
- Total: €250 and up

Keep in mind that during the high season (May–September), hotel and rental prices can increase significantly. Booking well in advance often helps secure better rates.

Budgeting Tips for Palma Travelers

- **Book early during peak season**: Prices for accommodations and tours rise fast in summer, especially in August.
- **Lunch menus (menú del día)**: Many restaurants offer a set lunch menu including starter, main course, dessert, and a drink for around €12–€18—a great value.
- **Use TIB and EMT buses**: Public transportation is reliable and affordable. A 10-trip ticket costs less per ride and can be used across Palma's urban buses.
- **Skip bottled water**: Tap water in Palma is safe to drink. Bring a reusable bottle and save money while reducing waste.

- **Visit markets and cook**: If you're staying in a rental with a kitchen, shop at local markets like Mercat de l'Olivar for fresh produce and cook your own meals occasionally.

Currency Exchange Services

Although not as common as in the past, currency exchange booths can still be found in the airport, city center, and around popular tourist spots. Exchange rates here are often less favorable than what you'd get via ATMs or your bank card.

Well-known locations include:

- **Global Exchange** (Airport)
- **Exact Change** (Palma center)
- **CaixaBank offices** with exchange counters

Always compare the offered rate and check for service fees before committing to an exchange.

Tipping Customs

Tipping in Palma is not obligatory, but it's appreciated for good service. Here's a rough guide:

- **Restaurants**: Round up the bill or leave 5–10% for excellent service
- **Bars and cafes**: Leave loose change or round up to the nearest euro
- **Taxis**: Round up the fare or tip €1–€2
- **Hotel staff**: €1–€2 for housekeeping or porter services
- **Tour guides**: €5–€10 depending on length and quality of the tour

Emergency Financial Situations

If you lose your card or run out of cash:

- **Western Union** and **MoneyGram** branches are available in Palma for emergency cash transfers.
- Contact your bank for a card replacement—some banks offer express delivery services.
- Keep a photocopy of your passport and card details stored safely (not on your phone) in case you need to contact your bank.

Being financially prepared while traveling in Palma means more than knowing the currency—it means understanding how to spend wisely, avoid fees, and make the most of your time without overspending. With thoughtful planning, you can balance comfort and cost-efficiency across your entire stay.

10.2 Language, Safety, and Emergency Info

Palma de Mallorca is a popular destination with a welcoming atmosphere, but being aware of the local language, safety practices, and emergency resources can make your visit smoother and more secure. Whether you're navigating healthcare or asking for directions, this section covers everything you need to know.

Languages Spoken in Palma

Official Languages:
Palma, like the rest of the Balearic Islands, recognizes **two official languages**:

- **Spanish (Castellano)**
- **Catalan (Mallorquín dialect)**

Mallorquín is a local variant of Catalan with its own vocabulary and pronunciation, but most locals are also fluent in Spanish. Catalan street signs, public notices, and announcements may appear alongside Spanish.

English Proficiency:
 Thanks to a strong tourism economy, **English is widely spoken** in Palma—especially in hotels, restaurants, airports, and shops in tourist areas. In more local neighborhoods or government offices, however, you may encounter limited English, so learning a few Spanish basics can go a long way.

Useful Spanish Phrases for Travelers:

- Hello: *Hola*
- Thank you: *Gracias*
- Please: *Por favor*
- Do you speak English?: *¿Habla inglés?*
- I need help: *Necesito ayuda*
- Where is the bathroom?: *¿Dónde está el baño?*

Locals appreciate the effort, even if it's just a greeting or thank you in their language.

General Safety in Palma

Palma is generally **a safe city**, with low levels of violent crime and a reputation for being traveler-friendly. As with any urban destination, basic precautions should be observed.

Crime and Scams:

- **Petty theft** is the most common issue, particularly **pickpocketing** in crowded areas such as bus stations, markets, and tourist-heavy zones like La Seu Cathedral or Paseo Marítimo.
- Keep your valuables secure and avoid carrying large amounts of cash or displaying expensive items like cameras or jewelry.
- Be cautious of **distraction tactics** used by thieves (like fake petitions or staged arguments).
- **ATM scams** can occur—use ATMs inside banks when possible and shield your PIN.

Nightlife Safety:
The nightlife scene is vibrant, especially in summer. Stick with your group, watch your drinks, and avoid unlicensed taxis late at night. Most venues close between 2:00–4:00 a.m., and police presence is common in busy nightlife zones.

Beach Safety:
Palma's beaches are clean and well-maintained, but take note of **flag warnings** that indicate sea conditions:

- Green: Safe to swim
- Yellow: Swim with caution
- Red: No swimming

Avoid leaving your belongings unattended while swimming, and consider using a beach-safe lockbox or dry bag for valuables.

Emergency Numbers and Services

Spain has a modern emergency response system. Dialing the appropriate number will connect you to English-speaking dispatchers in most cases.

Emergency Contacts:

- **112** – General Emergency (police, ambulance, fire)
- **091** – National Police (urban crime and security)
- **062** – Guardia Civil (rural and highway areas)
- **061** – Medical Emergency (ambulance services)
- **092** – Local Palma Police

Key Medical Facilities in Palma: If you require medical assistance beyond first aid, Palma has several excellent hospitals and clinics.

- **Son Espases University Hospital**
  Location: Ctra. de Valldemossa, 79, 07120 Palma
  Phone: +34 871 20 50 00
  Public hospital with modern facilities and emergency care.
- **Juaneda Hospital Palma**
  Location: C/ Company, 30, 07014 Palma
  Phone: +34 971 73 14 14
  A well-known private hospital with multilingual staff.

- **Clinica Rotger**

  Location: Carrer de Santiago Rusiñol, 9, 07012 Palma

  Phone: +34 971 44 33 00

  Centrally located private hospital offering a range of specialist services.

Pharmacies:

Pharmacies are abundant across the city and usually open during standard business hours. Look for a green cross sign. A rotating schedule ensures **at least one 24-hour pharmacy** is available per area. You can find the nearest one listed on the door of any pharmacy or through local apps.

Traveler Health and Insurance

- **No vaccinations** are required to enter Spain, but ensure your routine immunizations are up to date.
- **EU/EEA visitors** should bring a **European Health Insurance Card (EHIC)** or **EHIC replacement (GHIC)**.
- **Non-EU travelers** (including Americans and Canadians) should **have travel insurance** that includes emergency medical care and repatriation.
- Keep a copy of your insurance policy, a list of emergency contacts, and any prescriptions with you during travel.

Lost and Found, Tourist Support

- **Lost Items**: Lost property can be reported to the **Local Police** (Policía Local) or found at major transit hubs. Contact your hotel immediately if the item was lost on-premises.
- **Tourist Information Offices**: Staffed with multilingual representatives who can assist with directions, transportation, and general questions.
  - **Main Palma Tourism Office**

    Location: Parc de la Mar, near the Cathedral

    Phone: +34 971 72 22 16

    Open daily from 9:00 a.m. to 5:00 p.m.

Women and Solo Travel Safety

Palma is very accommodating for **solo travelers and women**, with generally low harassment levels. That said:

- Avoid walking alone through isolated areas at night.
- Use licensed taxis or rideshare apps when returning late from clubs or bars.
- Trust your instincts and avoid overly aggressive street vendors or promoters.

Natural Hazards and Weather Alerts

While Palma has mild weather year-round, it's wise to check for **seasonal risks**:

- **Heatwaves** (typically in July and August): Stay hydrated and avoid direct sun during peak hours (2–5 p.m.).
- **Heavy Rainfall or Coastal Storms** (rare but possible in autumn): Local authorities issue alerts via the **AEMET** weather service. These are posted in hotels, beaches, and public boards.

Being aware of your surroundings, knowing where to get help, and understanding the basics of local language and safety culture can make your visit to Palma both secure and stress-free. Up next is **10.3 Internet Access, SIM Cards, and Connectivity**, if you're ready to move on.

10.3 Accessibility and Family Travel

Palma de Mallorca is an increasingly inclusive destination, offering a welcoming atmosphere for travelers of all mobility levels and ages. Whether you're navigating the city in a wheelchair, traveling with a stroller, or managing a multi-generational family vacation, this section offers practical information to help you prepare and enjoy a smooth, accommodating stay.

Accessibility in Palma

General Infrastructure

Palma has made considerable progress in improving accessibility across its public spaces.

While historic areas like the Old Town can pose some challenges due to narrow cobblestone streets and elevation changes, many key attractions, public transportation options, and newer districts are well-equipped for travelers with limited mobility.

- **Pavements and Crossings**: Many sidewalks in central Palma have ramps at crossings and tactile paving for visually impaired pedestrians. Signalized pedestrian crossings are common in high-traffic areas.
- **Public Buildings**: Museums, government buildings, shopping centers, and most major attractions comply with European accessibility standards. These include ramps, wide doorways, elevators, and adapted restrooms.
- **Accessible Beaches**: Palma's beaches such as **Playa de Palma** and **Cala Major** provide **mobility matting**, **beach wheelchairs**, and **accessible bathrooms** during the high season.
- **Public Toilets**: Some city-maintained toilets are wheelchair-accessible. Look for signage indicating adapted facilities, especially in tourist zones and beaches.

Transport Accessibility

- **Airport**: Palma de Mallorca Airport (PMI) is fully accessible. It offers elevators, adapted toilets, reserved parking spots, and assistance services (booked in advance through your airline or Aena's website).
- **Buses**: EMT Palma buses are mostly equipped with **low-floor access**, **ramps**, and **priority seating**. They also include audiovisual stop announcements.
- **Taxis**: Palma has **adapted taxis (Eurotaxi)** available for wheelchair users. You can request one by calling local providers or through apps like TaxiClick or Radio Taxi Palma.
- **Rentals**: Companies like **Mallorca Adapted** and **Handisport Foundation** offer wheelchair-friendly car and equipment rentals (including scooters and walkers).

Attractions with Accessibility Options

- **La Seu Cathedral**: Wheelchair access is available via a separate entrance. There are elevators to key areas, and staff offer assistance on request.
- **Es Baluard Museum**: Fully accessible with ramps, lifts, and adapted bathrooms.
- **Bellver Castle**: The grounds and some exhibitions are accessible, though certain towers and walls may be limited due to their historical nature.

Family Travel in Palma

Palma is a fantastic family destination, blending cultural discovery with kid-friendly beaches, parks, and activities. Whether you're traveling with toddlers or teens, there's plenty to keep the whole family engaged and comfortable.

Accommodation for Families

Many hotels cater to families with amenities like:

- Family suites and interconnecting rooms
- Cribs and extra beds upon request
- Kids' clubs and babysitting services (especially in beach resorts)
- Pools with shallow zones or lifeguards
- On-site restaurants with child-friendly menus

Neighborhoods like **Playa de Palma**, **Portixol**, and **Santa Catalina** tend to have the best range of family-oriented lodging and dining.

Getting Around with Kids

- **Stroller Access**: While public transportation is stroller-friendly, Palma's Old Town has narrow, uneven streets. A lightweight or all-terrain stroller is recommended.
- **Child Safety**: Spanish car seat laws apply—children under 135 cm must use appropriate child restraints in vehicles. Some taxis may not carry child seats, so it's best to book in advance or bring your own.
- **Family Ticket Options**: EMT buses offer affordable rates, and some attractions provide family packages or reduced children's pricing.

Kid-Friendly Activities

- **Palma Aquarium**: One of the most popular attractions for families, featuring marine tanks, a tropical rainforest area, and interactive exhibits.
- **Beaches**: Playa de Palma and Can Pere Antoni have shallow water, soft sand, and beachside facilities like showers, playgrounds, and family cafés.
- **Parks**:
  - **Parc de la Mar** near the Cathedral offers plenty of space for running and shaded picnic areas.
  - **Parc de Ses Estacions** includes a playground, fountains, and open lawns.
- **Boat Tours**: Short glass-bottom boat rides around Palma Bay are great for keeping younger kids entertained.
- **Train to Sóller**: The vintage wooden train is a hit with kids and offers a scenic way to explore the island.

Dining with Children

- **Most restaurants in Palma welcome children**, and many provide high chairs, coloring menus, or kid-sized portions. Tapas bars may not have formal kids' menus but offer simple dishes like grilled chicken, bread with tomato, and omelets.
- **Ice Cream and Snack Stops**: Treats like gelato, churros, and pastries are widely available throughout the city.

Healthcare and Essentials for Families

- **Pediatric Care**: Public and private hospitals in Palma offer pediatric services. Emergency rooms usually include staff fluent in English or translators on call.
- **Pharmacies**: Stock a wide range of baby care items—formula, diapers, wipes, rash creams, and teething remedies. Ask for the *farmacia de guardia* (duty pharmacy) after hours.

- **Baby Supplies**: Supermarkets like Mercadona, Carrefour, and Lidl sell essentials like baby food, snacks, and nappies.

Travel Tips for Families and Travelers with Disabilities

- Book accessible accommodations or family suites **well in advance**, especially in summer.
- Carry a printed copy of **important Spanish phrases**, medical info, and allergy alerts.
- Use apps like **Google Maps**, **EMT Palma**, and **AccessAble** to check real-time info on transit and mobility access.
- Don't underestimate the **midday siesta culture**—many shops close between 2:00 and 5:00 p.m., which can be a great time for rest or quiet indoor activities with young children.

Palma is a city that continues to make strides in becoming more inclusive and family-friendly. With thoughtful planning, travelers of all needs and ages can enjoy a fulfilling and comfortable visit. Up next is **10.4 Sustainable and Responsible Tourism**, if you're ready to continue.

10.4 Useful Contacts and Resources

Whether you're preparing for your trip or already in Palma, having the right information at your fingertips can make your stay easier and safer. This section includes key contact numbers, important resources, online platforms, and helpful tools that travelers may need in a variety of situations—ranging from emergencies and public transport to tourist information and lost items.

Emergency Services

Spain uses a unified emergency response number, and response teams in Palma are well-equipped to handle calls in English.

- **Emergency Number (All services – Police, Ambulance, Fire):** 112
  (Free to call from any phone; available 24/7; multilingual)
- **Local National Police:** +34 971 77 11 00
- **Local Guardia Civil (rural and highway police):** +34 971 72 00 00
- **Palma Fire Department (Bomberos):** +34 971 72 61 92
- **Emergency Medical Services (SAMU 061):** 061 (or dial 112)

Hospitals and Medical Assistance

In case of illness or injury, Palma has both public and private medical facilities. Many doctors and staff speak English, particularly in private clinics.

Public Hospitals:

- **Hospital Universitari Son Espases**
  Address: Carrer de Valldemossa, 79, 07120 Palma
  Phone: +34 871 20 50 00
  Website: www.hospitalsonespases.es

Private Hospitals and Clinics:

- **Hospital Quirónsalud Palmaplanas**
  Address: Carrer de Camí dels Reis, 308, 07010 Palma
  Phone: +34 971 91 60 00
  Website: www.quironsalud.es
- **Juaneda Miramar Hospital**
  Address: Carrer de Camilo José Cela, 12, 07014 Palma
  Phone: +34 971 22 01 91
  Website: www.juaneda.es

Tourist Information

Palma's official tourism offices provide maps, brochures, guidance, and real-time help in multiple languages.

- **Main Tourist Office – Parc de la Mar**
  Address: Parc de la Mar, opposite La Seu Cathedral
  Phone: +34 971 17 61 12
  Email: informacioturisme@palma.cat
  Website: www.visitpalma.com
  Hours: Daily 9:00 a.m. – 2:00 p.m. (longer in summer)
- **Palma Airport Tourist Info Desk**
  Located in Arrivals Hall, PMI Airport
  Phone: +34 902 102 365
  Hours: Daily 9:00 a.m. – 8:00 p.m.

Transportation Contacts

Palma Airport (PMI):
Phone: +34 971 78 90 00
Website: www.aena.es

EMT Palma (City Buses):
Website: www.emtpalma.cat
Customer Service: +34 971 21 44 44
Real-time updates, timetables, and route planning available online and via mobile app.

Taxis (Radio Taxi Palma):
Phone: +34 971 40 14 14 or +34 971 73 00 40
App: TaxiClick Palma
Note: Accessible and family taxis available on request.

Train and Metro (SFM – Serveis Ferroviaris de Mallorca):
Phone: +34 971 17 77 77
Website: www.trensfm.com

Port of Palma (Cruise Terminal and Ferry Services):
Website: www.portsib.es
Ferry operators include Trasmed, Balearia, and GNV, with routes to mainland Spain and other Balearic Islands.

Consulates and Embassies

While Spain's main embassies are located in Madrid, several countries have consular services in Palma or nearby. Always check their websites for the most up-to-date hours and appointment policies.

- **British Consulate**
  Address: Calle Convent dels Caputxins 4, 07002 Palma
  Phone: +34 933 66 62 00
  Website: www.gov.uk
- **German Honorary Consulate**
  Address: Carrer de Sant Jaume 3, 07012 Palma
  Phone: +34 971 72 53 96
  Website: www.spanien.diplo.de
- **United States Consular Agency (Palma)**
  Address: Edificio Reina Constanza, Porto Pi, 07015 Palma
  Phone: +34 971 40 37 07
  Website: es.usembassy.gov

- **Canadian Consular Services**
  By appointment only, coordinated through Madrid
  Website: www.canadainternational.gc.ca

Lost and Found

- **Lost Items on EMT Buses**
  Phone: +34 971 21 44 44
  Email: info@emt.palma.cat
  Lost property is stored at EMT's main office.
- **Lost Items at Airport**
  Aena Lost and Found Office (Ground Floor Arrivals)
  Phone: +34 971 78 96 49
  Email: pmi.objetosperdidos@aena.es
- **Lost or Stolen Passport**
  Report immediately to the local police and contact your embassy or consulate.

Useful Apps and Online Tools

- **VisitPalma**: Official tourism app for attractions, maps, and guides
- **EMT Palma App**: For city buses—routes, real-time locations, and tickets
- **Google Maps**: Very reliable for walking, biking, and public transport routes
- **Moovit or Rome2Rio**: Great for planning longer trips or connections
- **TaxiClick**: Used for calling and tracking taxis in Palma
- **AccuWeather or AEMET**: Local weather updates

24-Hour Pharmacies and Late Services

- **Farmacia 24h – Farmacia Ramis**
  Address: Avinguda d'Alemanya, 7, 07003 Palma
  Phone: +34 971 72 21 66
- **Farmacia Llabrés 24h**
  Address: Avinguda Alexandre Rosselló, 36, 07002 Palma
  Phone: +34 971 72 06 25

Travel Insurance and Assistance

If you purchased travel insurance, keep your insurer's emergency contact card handy. Most insurers offer:

- 24-hour emergency hotlines
- Assistance with hospital admission

- Evacuation or repatriation support
- Reimbursement for lost items or trip cancellations

For European Union travelers, the **European Health Insurance Card (EHIC)** is valid in public hospitals but doesn't cover private services or repatriation—additional insurance is still recommended.

Whether you're planning ahead or navigating an unexpected issue while on the island, having these resources at the ready ensures greater peace of mind. Palma is a friendly, well-organized city with strong infrastructure in place to support all kinds of travelers.

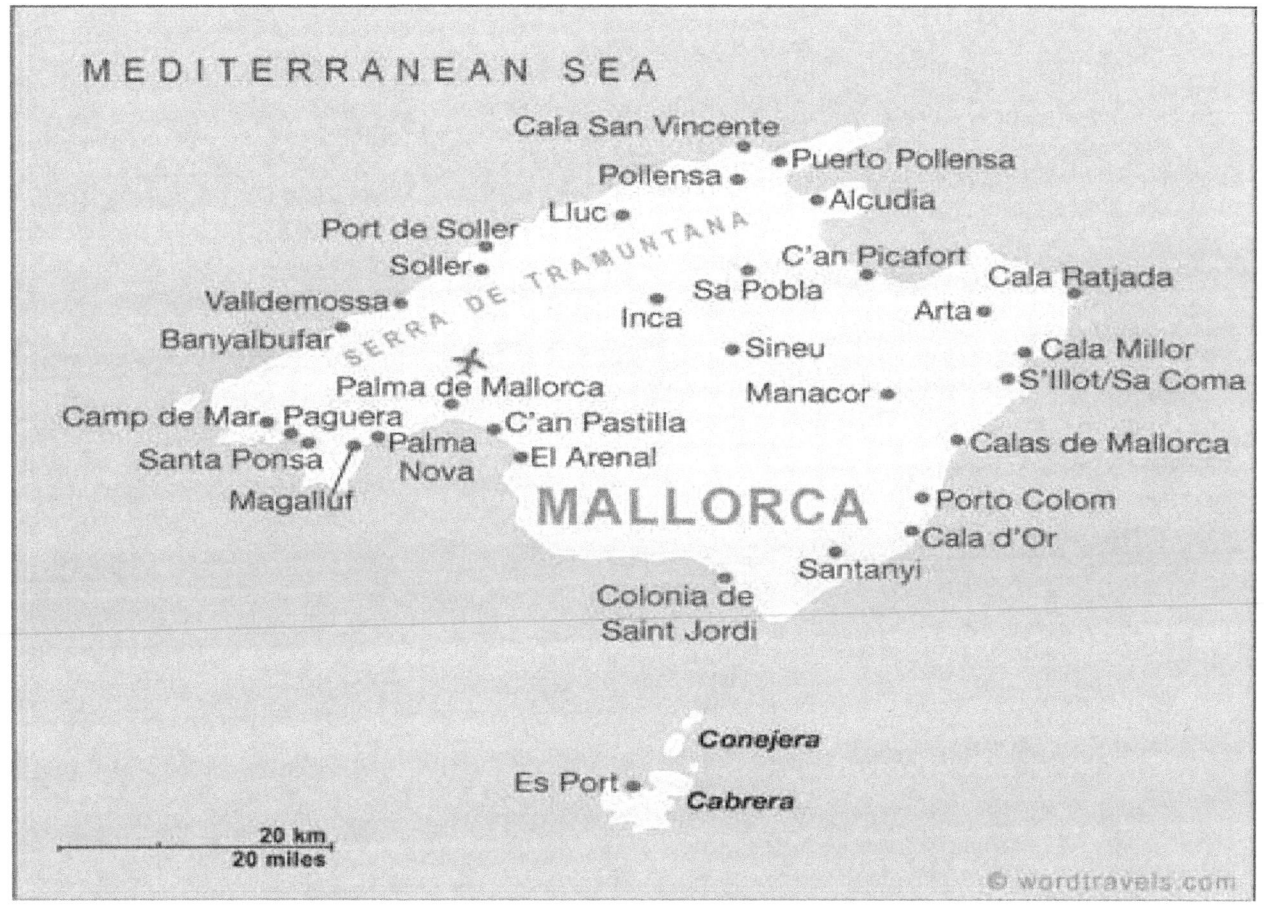

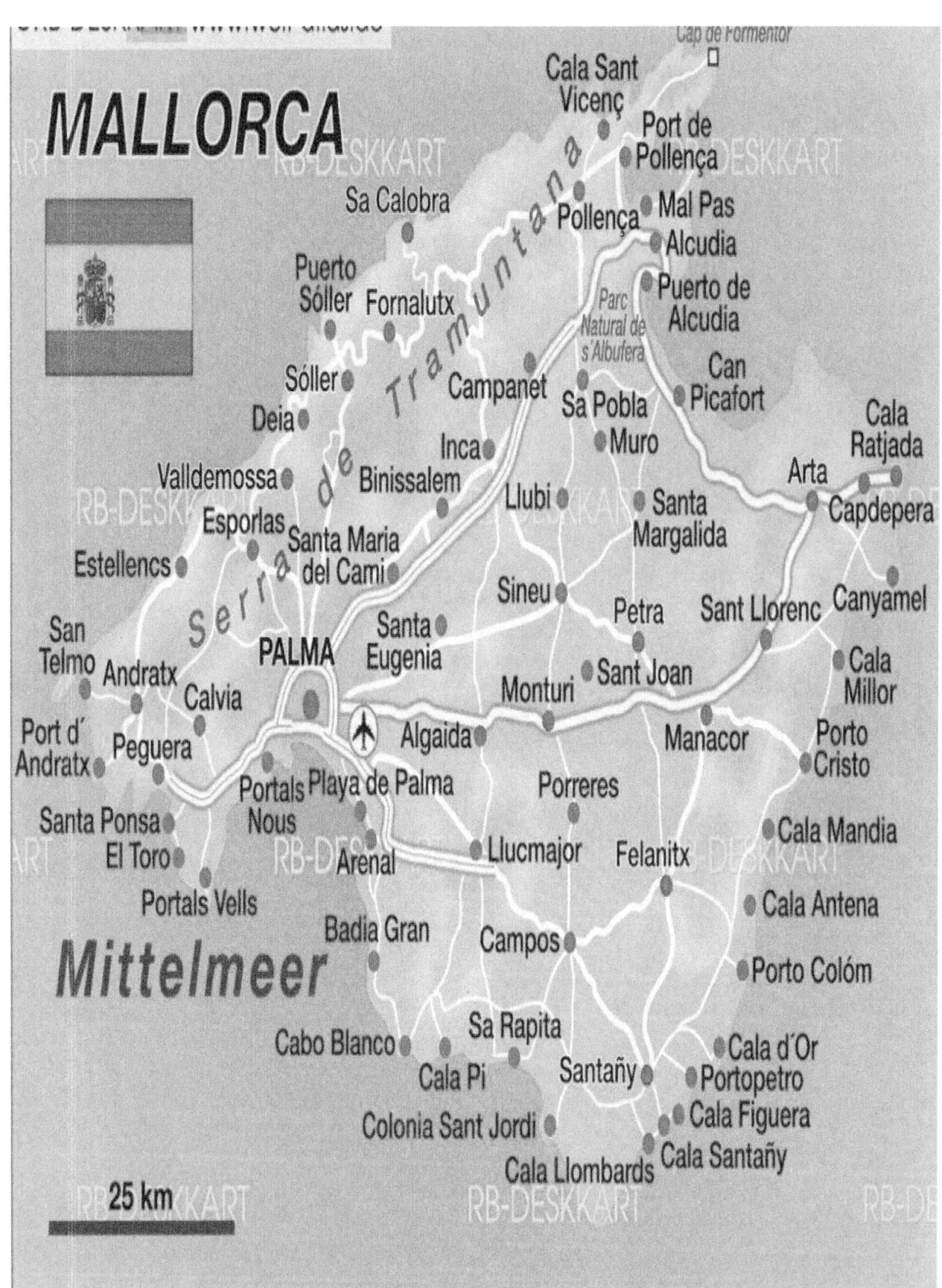

MALLORCA

Cap de Formentor

Cala Sant Vicenç

Port de Pollença

Sa Calobra

Pollença

Mal Pas

Alcudia

Puerto Sóller

Fornalutx

Parc Natural de s'Albufera

Puerto de Alcudia

Can Picafort

Cala Ratjada

Sóller

Campanet

Sa Pobla

Deia

Muro

Arta

Valldemossa

Inca

Binissalem

Llubi

Santa Margalida

Capdepera

Esporlas

Santa Maria del Cami

Sineu

Petra

Sant Llorenc

Canyamel

Estellencs

San Telmo

Andratx

Calvia

PALMA

Santa Eugenia

Monturi

Sant Joan

Manacor

Cala Millor

Porto Cristo

Serra de Tramuntana

Port d´ Andratx

Peguera

Algaida

Portals Nous

Playa de Palma

Porreres

Santa Ponsa

El Toro

Arenal

Llucmajor

Felanitx

Cala Mandia

Portals Vells

Badia Gran

Campos

Cala Antena

Porto Colóm

Mittelmeer

Cabo Blanco

Sa Rapita

Cala Pi

Santañy

Cala d'Or

Portopetro

Colonia Sant Jordi

Cala Figuera

Cala Llombards

Cala Santañy

25 km

Printed in Dunstable, United Kingdom